We Move
Our Own Cheese!

Also available from ASQ Quality Press:

Making Change in Complex Organizations
George K. Strodtbeck III

Lean Acres: A Tale of Strategic Innovation and Improvement in a Familiar Setting
Jim Bowie

Making Change Work: Practical Tools for Overcoming Human Resistance to Change
Brien Palmer

Office Kaizen: Transforming Office Operations into a Strategic Competitive Advantage
William Lareau

The Executive Guide to Improvement and Change
G. Dennis Beecroft, Grace L. Duffy, John W. Moran

The Quality Toolbox, Second Edition
Nancy R. Tague

Root Cause Analysis: Simplified Tools and Techniques, Second Edition
Bjørn Andersen and Tom Fagerhaug

The Certified Six Sigma Green Belt Handbook, Second Edition
Roderick A. Munro, Govindarajan Ramu, and Daniel J. Zrymiak

The Certified Manager of Quality/Organizational Excellence Handbook, Fourth Edition
Russell T. Westcott, editor

The Certified Six Sigma Black Belt Handbook, Third Edition
T.M. Kubiak and Donald W. Benbow

The ASQ Auditing Handbook, Fourth Edition
J.P. Russell, editor

The ASQ Quality Improvement Pocket Guide: Basic History, Concepts, Tools, and Relationships
Grace L. Duffy, editor

To request a complimentary catalog of ASQ Quality Press publications, call 800-248-1946, or visit our Web site at http://www.asq.org/quality-press.

We Move Our Own Cheese!

A Business Fable About Championing Change

Victor E. Sower and
Frank K. Fair

ASQ Quality Press
Milwaukee, Wisconsin

American Society for Quality, Quality Press, Milwaukee, WI 53203
© 2017 by ASQ.
All rights reserved. Published 2017.
Printed in the United States of America.

22   21   20   19   18   17   5   4   3   2

Library of Congress Cataloging in Publication
Control Number: 2016055676

Director of Products, Quality Programs: Ray Zielke
Managing Editor: Paul Daniel O'Mara
Sr. Creative Services Specialist: Randy L. Benson

ASQ Mission: The American Society for Quality advances individual, organizational, and community excellence worldwide through learning, quality improvement, and knowledge exchange.

Attention Bookstores, Wholesalers, Schools, and Corporations: ASQ Quality Press books, video, audio, and software are available at quantity discounts with bulk purchases for business, educational, or instructional use. For information, please contact ASQ Quality Press at 800-248-1946, or write to ASQ Quality Press, P.O. Box 3005, Milwaukee, WI 53201-3005.

To place orders or to request ASQ membership information, call 800-248-1946. Visit our Web site at www.asq.org/quality-press.

∞ Printed on acid-free paper

Quality Press
600 N. Plankinton Ave.
Milwaukee, WI 53203-2914
E-mail: authors@asq.org

The Global Voice of Quality®

Contents

List of Figures and Tables

Acknowledgments

The authors thank the following individuals who read early drafts of our fable and provided encouragement, valuable feedback, and suggestions for ways we could improve the manuscript.

- Ms. Jerrine Baker, M. B. A., lecturer of Management and Marketing, Sam Houston State University and president/owner, Majestic Dreams Travel

- Mr. Peter Birkholz, M. B. A., managing partner, Sam Houston Group, LP and management consultant, Birkholz Management Co., LLC

- Mr. Richard Bozeman, author and inventor, retired chief of the Propulsion and Power Division Test Facilities, NASA

- Ms. Janet Fair, M. Ed. and English M. A., academic mentor and retired educator

- Mr. Kenneth Fair, J. D., partner, Wright & Close LLP

- Dr. Kenneth Green, Ph. D., Lemay professor of Management, Southern Arkansas University

- Dr. Geraldine Hynes, Ph. D., professor of Business Communication, Sam Houston State University

- Dr. Scott Kaukonen, Ph. D., director of the MFA Creative Writing Program, Sam Houston State University

- Dr. Juliana Lilly, Ph. D., professor of Management, Sam Houston State University

- Mr. Christopher Sower, M. B. A., C. P. S. M., C. P. M., vice president, Americas and West Africa Logistics, Nalco Champion, An Ecolab Company and president, Sower & Associates, LLC

- Ms. Judy Sower, M. Ed., author and retired educator

- Dr. Pamela Zelbst, Ph. D., P. M. P., associate professor of Operations Management, director of Sower Business Technology, and director of the Center for Innovation & Technology, Sam Houston State University

We also acknowledge and thank Matt Meinholz, acquisitions editor, Paul O'Mara, managing editor, the entire ASQ Quality Press production staff, and the three anonymous ASQ Quality Press reviewers for their feedback and suggestions.

Prologue

WE MOVE OUR OWN CHEESE!

THE MORAL OF THE STORY: The need to create change—to move from being an extreme risk-averse, head-in-the-sand, reactive organization to becoming an insightful organization that recognizes the necessity of creating change and taking risks in order to survive and thrive.

Have you ever felt that you had a great insight that would benefit your department, division, or organization and found that you seem to be the only one who can see it? Worse yet, has it ever seemed that while you are struggling to pull your idea into consideration, others are actively holding you back? If you just had the power, you think, great things could be accomplished.

What is your reaction? Have you and others who suggest new ideas been so beaten down in the past that you simply let the idea go because it isn't worth the emotional capital to pursue it? If that is the case, and your idea is indeed a good one, who suffers? You? The organization? The organization's customers? The answer is all of the above.

This book is designed to help those with limited positional power to find ways to get their ideas seriously considered. It is also designed to help those with positional power create a culture that encourages ideas that will benefit the organization regardless of their source.

We have been inspired by Spencer Johnson's classic fable, *Who Moved My Cheese?*[1] Johnson's book imparts an important message in a simple, easy to understand, and entertaining way. The message is about how to deal with change in your personal and professional life. We have been inspired by its message both personally and professionally.

The four main lessons in Johnson's book are:

1. Change Happens (They keep moving the cheese)

2. Anticipate Change (Get ready for the cheese to move)

3. Monitor Change (Smell the cheese often so you know when it is getting old)

4. Adapt to Change Quickly (The quicker you let go of old cheese the sooner you can enjoy new cheese)

The idea for this book, *We Move Our Own Cheese!*, was developed over a discussion about Johnson's book. We decided that there was another story that could be told about taking a more proactive, team-based approach to change. As Johnson's book points out, individuals must be agile enough to effectively react to change in order to survive. This is just as true for organizations. However, the best individuals and organizations create change more often than they react to it. The founders of Apple Computer created change by developing and marketing a personal computer that pioneered excellent graphics and the graphical user interface. After a pause, Apple continued to create change with the iPod, iPad, iPhone, and Apple Watch. Motorola created change by developing the Six Sigma approach to quality. IBM created change by developing and leasing mainframe computers and serving as one of the pioneers in personal computing.

The best way to predict the future is to create it.

PETER DRUCKER

We Move Our Own Cheese! is about creating change. As in Johnson's book, the cheese is a metaphor for what we have in life and what we believe we want more of. In a business context, it represents the business we are in—our current paradigm—and what it gives us. However, as Richard Pascal said, "The incremental approach to change is (only) effective when what you want is more of what you've already got."[2] Individuals and organizations often think they want more of what they already have. The slide rule manufacturers of the 1960s thought their new cheese would come from larger markets for slide rules. But the bigger opportunity was the electronic calculator and personal computer (PC) markets. Failure to recognize that opportunity resulted in the demise of the slide rule manufacturers. Dell Computer has gone from a publicly traded company to a privately owned one and is currently struggling with how to react to a declining PC market. What organizations in similar situations should be seeking is not more of the cheese they currently have, but ways to create their own new cheese. In our story the new cheese becomes a strategic metaphor representing what we should really strive for—an innovative strategic objective—in order to survive and thrive.

Creating your own cheese is not the end of the story. Organizations often go through a life cycle described by the technology S-curve (Figure 1). They start with a great idea that grows but eventually begins to lose steam. The first response by the organization may be denial—"If we just increase our marketing budget, we will never run out of cheese." The next response might be, "If we just make some improvements to our current products, we will never run out of cheese." Sometimes these approaches work—but sometimes they do not. Photography pioneer Kodak and bookseller Borders found out the hard way that regardless of increased marketing investments and incremental improvements, their cheese did run out.

In order to cope with diminishing cheese supply (maturity stage), organizations must seek to take control over their environment. They must move beyond incremental improvement (where do we find new stocks of cheese) to creating their own new cheese. These proactive organizations can be described by a series of S-curves as shown in Figure 2.

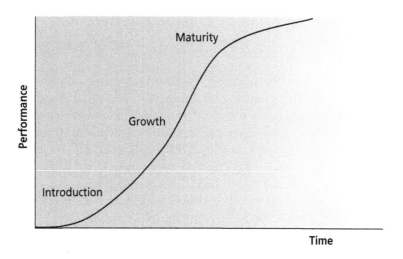

Figure 1 The technology S-curve.[3]

We have to try new things all the time because the innovation cycle is shortening. Timeliness is more important.

PATRICK WOHLHAUSER[4]

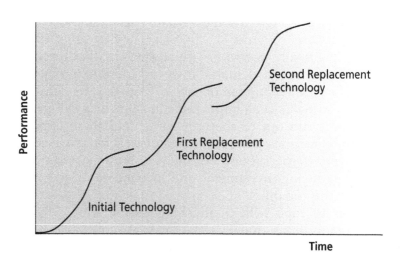

Figure 2 Replacement technologies and S-curves.[5]

Seeking to make your own cheese is not without risk of failure. Resources may be invested in projects that are dead ends—failures. But best-in-class organizations embrace risk, regarding failure as an opportunity to learn. In the words of Samuel Beckett, "Try again. Fail again. Fail better."[6] Leading organizations embrace uncertainty because that is where the next great thing is to be found. As Pete Athans, the alpinist who has successfully climbed Mt. Everest several times, puts it, "There's no magic to getting where we already know we can go."[7]

Our book focuses on just one theme while acknowledging that there are many other reasons why companies do not realize their potential or even fail. Enron, the original DeLorean, and, more recently, a number of oil production-related companies failed for quite different reasons than those addressed in our book. We contend, though, that all companies can benefit from the message in our book, whether they aspire to create new cheese while competitors struggle to keep up or simply recognize the new cheese created elsewhere and be among the first to take advantage of it.

In our story the Community represents a corporation or other organization established years ago by an innovative and charismatic Founder. The organization is naturally risk-averse and tradition-bound, often taking a "What would the Founder do?" approach to major decisions. The Elders represent top management. The Chief Elder in Office is, of course, the CEO.

Our protagonist, Visio, and his friends represent low- to mid-level professional employees of the organization. Visio becomes a champion for profound organizational change. The maze is the environment in which the organization exists. Initially the organization does not control its interactions with the maze—the larger environment—and actually fears it. And their vitally important cheese is just mysteriously present. Our story is about how the organization gains control over its interactions with the larger environment by learning to create its own cheese.

Mr. Philo, the librarian, represents a long-tenured professional employee of the organization who is a friend and an unofficial mentor to Visio.

The Dead Community Visio's team encounters represents an organization that could not adapt to change and ceased to exist.

The newly discovered other community, the Village, represents a potential supply chain partner to the Community.

The story represents how an organization transforms itself (kicking and screaming) from reactive—reacting to changes in its environment (cheese supply)—to proactive—actually creating changes in its environment. The community moves from an external to an internal locus of control. Consequently, the upshot of our fable can be expressed as:

> *It is better to create your own change than to react*
> *to change created by others.*

However, this main lesson grows out of a number of contributing lessons:

- Sometimes you find important things when you aren't looking for them.

- Simply pointing out a problem is unlikely to result in action.

- If you propose a radical new idea, don't be surprised if some of your colleagues do not back you.

- It takes more than facts and a plan to convince decision makers of the need to change.

- The most fearsome thing is the unknown.

- There is risk of failure associated with exploring the unknown, but we can learn much from our failure.

- We have to be open-minded about things that are new to us.

- We must be careful not to allow our fears to blind us to the potential good that might result from our encounter with the unknown.

- Those in charge do not like public surprises.

- Associates aren't always as loyal as they seem.

- Debacles can sometimes be sources of opportunities.

- It is wise to weigh the risks associated with doing nothing and compare them to the risks of deciding to take action.

- Seeking out diverse experiences can prepare you for dealing with unpredictable challenges.

- Just when you think you've got things all mapped out, they can change; when they do, new thinking is needed to deal with the change.

We hope that you enjoy the journey that our hero, Visio, must go through to change his Community and that you can find parallels in your own experiences with trying to move an organization forward to where it needs to be.

1

A Discovery

Visio gazed up at the statue of the Founder while he waited in line for the weekly distribution of cheese. Few in the Community remembered the Founder who had been gone for many years. However, he still exerted significant influence on the Community and its members. Details are sketchy, but everyone knew that the Founder had discovered cheese and established the Community to benefit from it. He had established the rules by which the Community carefully preserves and maintains the cheese supply and allocates it among its members. Whenever a significant decision is to be made, the Council of Elders always asks "What would the Founder do?" The answer to that question guides the decision, a process that has provided stability and prosperity for the Community and its members for many years.

The Community was founded more than forty years ago. No one is sure where the Founder came from, but it was from somewhere in the maze within which the Community exists. The Community is dominated by the very large Cheese Warehouse. Next to the Warehouse is the community square where members gather on special occasions and for the weekly distribution of cheese. Surrounding the square are other community buildings such as the Library and the Hall of the Elders. Beyond the square are the modest dwellings of the members.

Suddenly Visio heard a loud crash and turned just in time to see one of the Elders charged with distributing the cheese rations fall as he carried a large box of cheese from the warehouse. Instinctively, Visio vaulted over the table and rushed to provide aid to the fallen Elder. He helped the Elder to his feet and reached to pick up the box of cheese. As he did so, he looked through the door into the Warehouse. No one but the Elders has been allowed in the Cheese Warehouse, so this was a rare opportunity for Visio to satisfy his curiosity about what was inside. Visio was startled to see that the warehouse was huge, and he saw tall stacks of cheese in the far end of the warehouse. Other Elders quickly arrived to help the fallen Elder and hustled Visio to the other side of the table where he rejoined the line. While he waited for his turn, he made a mental note to make an entry in his diary about his helping the fallen Elder and his peek into the Cheese Warehouse.

Visio finally received his cheese ration. The Elders have dispensed the weekly cheese ration since the days of the Founder. It is as regular as clockwork. Visio was content that there had always been sufficient cheese available for everyone in the Community since the days of the Founder, and he believed that there would always be more cheese. Then he was off to meet his friends for lunch.

The friends had met at the Library some years ago in chance encounters. Since so few people used the Library, those who did naturally gravitated together. But what had really cemented the relationship among the friends was the disaster at the Bicycle Shop. When the roof collapsed, the owners, Orville and Wilber, needed help repairing it. Visio and his six friends offered their help. A few weeks later, the Bicycle Shop was in better repair than ever. The friends had found that they enjoyed working together—each bringing his or her skill set to the team.

During lunch at the restaurant Visio could not wait to share his experience at the Cheese Warehouse. He met with six of his closest friends and talked about having assisted the fallen Elder with as much humility as he could muster. Almost as an afterthought, he mentioned what he saw in the Warehouse. "It was amazing—so big!" exclaimed Visio.

"What else did you see?" came the chorus from his friends.

"Well, it was huge with tall stacks of cheese at the far end," replied Visio, a bit chagrined that his friends seemed to care more about the Warehouse than his "heroic" feat.

"What else did you see?" Cassandra asked.

"There wasn't much else to see. I didn't have a long look inside. I was too busy helping the Elder," replied Visio.

"I wonder what they use the front of the Warehouse for?" asked Logio.

"Good question, Logio. I wonder if it ever was filled with cheese," Cassandra said.

Mauri chimed in, "That's a big building. It could hold a lot of cheese. How much cheese do you think was there, Visio? If it was once filled with cheese, where did it go?"

Cassandra jumped in. "Do you think we could ever run out of cheese? What would we do?"

"Wait! Wait!" exclaimed Visio. "I saw a lot of cheese in the warehouse. We must be fine or the Elders would tell us. They would be working on finding new cheese."

The clock in the square chimed 12:00. "Oh, I am meeting with a friend at the Library. I'm late. I must run." said Visio. He bade goodbye to his friends and headed to the Library. Visio enjoyed spending time at the Library. Not only did he find interesting books to read there, but he had also grown close to the Librarian, Mr. Philo. Mr. Philo was among the oldest members of the Community and in fact one of the few who could say he actually knew the Founder. When Mr. Philo was a young boy, he had worked in the Founder's library after school. Over the years he had held several positions within the Community, but he had always maintained the Library. Now, maintaining the Library is all that he does.

Very few members of the Community frequent the Library, so one of Mr. Philo's main jobs is dusting the stacks of books. That gives him plenty of time to tell Visio stories about the early days of the Community. Today, Visio was eager to tell a story of his own about what happened at the Cheese Warehouse.

After hearing the story, Mr. Philo praised Visio for his readiness to help the Elder, but then Visio said, "The Elders seemed troubled that I had seen inside the Cheese Warehouse. But there was nothing to see. Just some cheese stacked at the far back of the Warehouse. Some of my friends wondered what they used the front part of the Warehouse for, and none of us could come up with an answer."

Mr. Philo allowed, "When I was a young man I once saw the inside of the Warehouse when I was assigned to build storage racks to hold the weekly cheese ration. In those days the Warehouse was almost full."

"Some of my friends are afraid that we may be running out of cheese. Cassandra asked whether the front of the Warehouse had once been filled with cheese. Why do you think the front part is now empty?" asked Visio.

"The Elders are in charge of the cheese. Only they can answer that question," said Mr. Philo with a shrug.

"Do you think what I saw is important enough to talk to the Elders about? I wasn't even trying to see inside the Warehouse. It just happened," said Visio.

Mr. Philo paused thoughtfully for a minute. "Sometimes you find important things when you are not looking for them. You will never know whether what you saw is important or not if you just forget about it."

As Visio began the walk home from the Library, Mr. Philo's words kept whirling around in his mind. If the Community was running out of cheese, it would be very important to be sure the Elders were aware of it. He sat down on a bench in the square to make an entry in his diary and then continued his trek home.

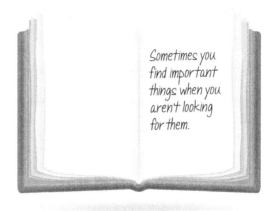

Sometimes you find important things when you aren't looking for them.

On his way home Visio stopped at the coffee bar in the lobby of the Council House. An Elder sat at a table near the door. Visio asked the barista, "Who is the Elder sitting over there?"

The barista whispered "That is the Chief Elder in Office—the CEO. He often stops in here for a cappuccino on his way out of the office in the evening."

Mr. Philo had said that only the Elders could answer his question, thought Visio. On impulse, Visio went over to the CEO's table just as the man stood up to leave. "Sir," blurted Visio in a voice a little higher pitched than normal, "I am sorry to bother you, but I have an important question to ask you. It's about something I saw this morning and it may concern the very existence of the Community. It's about the cheese supply. This morning I accidentally saw inside the Warehouse, and it looked to me that the Warehouse was only partly full. I am afraid that if things continue as they are we might run out of cheese. What would we do then?"

The CEO frowned, and he took a serious tone with Visio. "Mr.—eh, who did you say you were?"

"I didn't, sir. My name is Visio."

"Well, Mr. Visio, the Founder provided the cheese for the Community and the Elders administer the Community just as the Founder would. We have always had plenty of cheese. There is no problem. Now, if you will excuse me, I must go." With that he left.

A somewhat dejected Visio picked up his coffee and found an empty table. "Well, that didn't go so well," he thought. As he sat there he made a second diary entry. It was very unusual for Visio to find more than one thing a day worthy of noting in his diary.

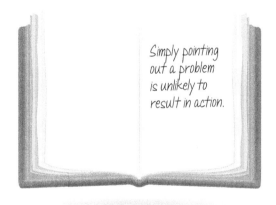

Simply pointing out a problem is unlikely to result in action.

2

Preparing the Case

The next morning Visio could not wait to talk with his friends again about the Cheese Warehouse. "Mr. Philo says only the Elders can answer our questions about the empty space in the Cheese Warehouse," said Visio. "I tried to talk with the CEO yesterday in the coffee bar, but he said there wasn't a problem with the cheese supply, so maybe I should just forget about it."

"Well, that's that," said Bromo. "Let's just forget about it."

"How can we do that?" voiced Cassandra.

"Yeah, how can we just forget about it?" chimed in Logio and Mauri. Bromo and the other two friends remained silent.

"I think Cassandra and Logio are right," said Visio. "I just wasn't very prepared to talk with the CEO yesterday in the coffee bar. That's why the CEO didn't listen to me. But I saw a notice in the coffee bar in the Council House that there is an open meeting in two weeks where community members can ask the Elders questions. I think we should gather data and put together a presentation to document the problem that the cheese supply may fail."

"Aren't you afraid to ask the Elders such a question? What if they are offended? What then for us?" asked Cassandra.

"But it is an open meeting. Community members are free to say what they want in an open meeting, aren't they? If we collect data that supports our concern and present a plan to deal with it, the Elders will listen to us. Perhaps they will even reward us for pointing out the potential cheese supply problem," said Visio.

"Perhaps, but I have a bad feeling about this," said Casssandra. "No one questions the Elders. They are in charge of all decisions affecting the Community. What if they don't like our asking about the Cheese Warehouse? What if they punish you for even seeing inside the Warehouse? No one but the Elders is allowed access. What if...?"

Visio cut her off. "Cassandra! I didn't sneak into the Warehouse. I accidentally saw the inside when I helped the Elder. Why would they punish me for that? Surely they will be willing to tell us what they are doing to make sure we do not run out of cheese. What's to fear? Now who wants to help me collect the data we need?"

Bromo and two of the other friends excused themselves, offering reasons why they would be unable to help. "Well, I didn't expect that," said Visio. Only Cassandra, Mauri, and Logio remained. "What about you? Will you help me?" A bit hesitantly, they agreed to help.

With that, the four friends planned their next step. They all agreed that they must be well prepared for the open meeting. "Who am I to them? Just another member of the Community," said Visio.

So the friends decided: "Data are what we need to convince them to listen to us. We have to have data to support our concern that we might be running out of cheese."

They needed data. But what data? "What we need is an estimate of how much cheese we started with, how much we have left, and how long it will last," said Visio. Mauri had good skills as a mapmaker, so he agreed to pace off the dimensions of the Cheese Warehouse and create a scale diagram showing its volume. Using an estimate of the empty space based on what Visio had seen, they could then estimate the remaining volume that was still filled with cheese.

Cassandra agreed to consult with Mr. Philo to find census records so that they could document how many members had been fed from the cheese supply since the founding of the Community. Logio agreed to estimate the growth rate of the colony. Visio would take all of the information and estimate how long the remaining cheese supply would last.

After a few days the four friends met to put it all together. The conclusion was that there was sufficient cheese remaining for just five more years with the current rates of population growth and individual consumption.

"Now we have the data we need," exclaimed Visio. "The Elders will have to listen to us."

"Perhaps we should prepare the data so that it is easy to see what we have done," suggested Logio.

"Yes," Mauri volunteered, "We need charts and graphs. I can do those."

A few days later the four friends met again in the park. Visio, Cassandra, and Logio admired Mauri's charts (Figure 3). "Just what we need to document the problem," allowed Visio, "but what should we do about it?"

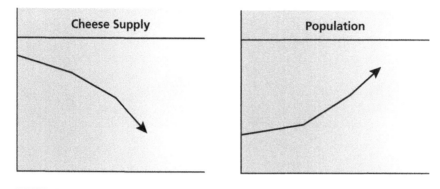

Figure 3 Mauri's graphs.

Logio was the first to speak. "We know there is no cheese in the Community except in the Cheese Warehouse. So, unless we can come up with a way to multiply the cheese we already have, we must find new cheese."

After further discussion, the four friends felt that they were stuck. None of their ideas seemed to be right for addressing the problem. "The next open meeting is in one week. We don't have much time to develop a plan. Why don't we go to the Library and see if Mr. Philo can help us?" said Visio.

Mr. Philo was impressed with all of the work the four friends had done. In response to their request for help, he told them "I'll see what I can do, but this might take a while."

Unwilling to "wait a while," Visio said, "We have the data. It is the Elders who must develop the plan. Once we present the data it will certainly convince the Elders that there is a problem with the cheese supply and they will develop a plan," said Visio. "Now let's go celebrate at the coffee shop."

Visio was so excited about the presentation they had prepared for the Elders that he couldn't go to sleep that night. He thought back over the excitement of getting the presentation ready, but he also couldn't stop thinking about how Bromo and some of the others friends had been so reluctant to help. He pulled out his diary and made an entry for the day. "I can't wait for the open meeting next week." With that, he was finally able to go to sleep.

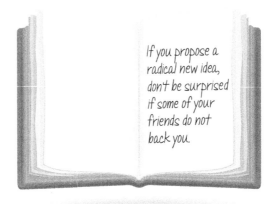

If you propose a radical new idea, don't be surprised if some of your friends do not back you.

3

The First Meeting
with the Elders

A week later, the evening for the open meeting had arrived. Visio, Logio, Mauri, and Cassandra approached the Council House dressed in their finest apparel. They made their way inside and found a seat near the back of the room. Others, mostly older residents of the Community, slowly filed in until the room was about half full.

"All rise!" bellowed the Herald from the front of the room. Immediately the Elders filed into the room and took their seats behind the long table on the stage at the front of the room. Behind them, on a slightly raised platform, the CEO took his seat. "Be seated!" intoned the Herald.

As everyone took their seats, the first Elder read his remarks. This took at least fifteen minutes. One by one, each of the Elders took his turn reading his remarks. After about two hours, the last Elder finished his remarks and all was quiet.

Then the Herald's voice boomed "Are there any questions for the Elders?" For what seemed like a long time, no one moved. Finally one of the older Community members present rose to be recognized. "I would like to thank the Elders for sharing all of this information with the Community." Then he sat down, and it appeared that no one else had a question.

Taking a deep breath, Visio stood up and was recognized. Struggling to clear his throat, Visio began, "A few days ago while helping an Elder who had fallen, I accidentally saw the inside of the Cheese Warehouse. I saw that it was largely empty. After talking with my friends, we are concerned that we might be running out of cheese."

Everyone in the room turned to look at Visio. The Community members' faces reflected surprise that a young member would say such a thing to the Elders. While several of the Elders exchanged glances, most stared directly at Visio—their faces seemingly turned to stone. Visio couldn't help shivering a bit.

"My friends and I decided that we needed to assess the risk of the Community running out of cheese by collecting data," Visio said as Logio held up the charts (Figure 4) Mauri had prepared. "Our data show that the consumption of cheese is consistent with the empty space in the Warehouse. The population in the Community is growing rapidly, which means we will run out of cheese in our lifetimes. We estimate there are only five years of cheese left."

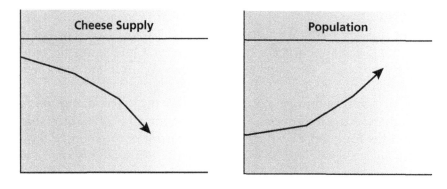

Figure 4 Mauri's graphs.

Finally the CEO spoke. "It is Mr. Visio, isn't it?"

"Yes sir," Visio responded. "We met earlier this week in the coffee bar."

"Mr. Visio, you know that only the Elders may see inside of the Cheese Warehouse. It is forbidden for Community members to access it. We will overlook this violation since it occurred as you were helping one of the Elders. As for the cheese supply, your data are interesting. However, the cheese was provided by the Founder. We do not question the wisdom of the Founder."

"But sir," Visio continued, "the data are clear. You must develop a plan to address the problem!"

A collective gasp was heard throughout the room.

"Mr. Visio, we have already told you that there is not a problem with the cheese supply. Your data must be wrong. The Founder has provided. There has always been enough cheese for the Community." With that, the Chief Elder beckoned to the Herald.

The Herald droned, "All rise" and the meeting was dismissed. Most of the Elders left the room immediately, but Visio noticed that that the small group of Elders who exchanged glances when he presented the problem stayed in their seats talking among themselves.

All of the Community members in attendance pointedly avoided Visio and his friends as they left the Council House. As the friends walked home, they discussed what had happened in the meeting with the Elders. "Perhaps Bromo and the others were right. Perhaps we should have stayed quiet about this," said Visio.

"No!" Cassandra almost shouted. "We failed tonight, but failure is an opportunity to learn. We four are convinced that the cheese supply is in danger. We know that something has to be done. We are the only ones willing to consider that. We have to analyze what happened tonight and find another way to convince the Elders that we are right. We can't just drop this. It is too important."

Cassandra had revitalized the group. They all agreed to think about what happened and to meet at the Library the next day to develop a plan. They were to consider ways to convince the Elders to accept their analysis and to do something about the cheese supply.

When he arrived home, Visio turned what had happened over in his mind. Within minutes, he was asleep on the sofa.

4

The Second Meeting
with the Elders

The four friends met at the Library to discuss the previous day's events and to decide what they would do next. Before they could get far, Mr. Philo passed by on his way to his office.

"Good morning Visio, Cassandra, Mauri, and Logio. I heard about the meeting last night. You displayed great courage making a presentation to the Elders," Mr. Philo said cheerily.

"But they didn't believe us," said Visio. "We have made no progress at all."

"We even considered dropping the whole thing after the meeting," Logio said. "But we decided it was too important for that. The more we study the problem, the more we realize how important it is. I don't know why the Elders haven't already seen it and taken action to insure the cheese supply for years to come."

"I heard the whole story about last night," said Mr. Philo. "From what I understand, you had excellent data about the problem, but you proposed no plan to deal with it. You also didn't take into account that the Elders have been making decisions the same way almost since the founding of the Community. They aren't used to members asking questions that might be interpreted as criticism. It often takes more than facts to convince people to change, especially when they have been doing things successfully for a long time. You need a plan and a way to convince the Elders to support your plan. Perhaps I can help you with the latter, but only you can formulate a plan."

The four friends agreed almost in unison. "You're right! A plan! We can't wait for the Elders, we must create a plan!"

Visio's sense of elation was more short-lived than the others. "Yeah, a plan. But what plan? What do we know about planning? That's the Elders' job."

"Maybe it isn't just the Elders who must plan," said Cassandra. "After all, no one can be smart enough or wise enough to see everything and plan for everything. I think everyone in the Community should have a role in making plans. After all, we are all in the Community together. The Elders and members receive the same cheese from the same source. If the Elders aren't willing to plan, then we must!"

"But where would we ever find more cheese?" asked Logio. "We know all of the ins and outs of the Community. There just isn't any more cheese outside the Warehouse."

"The Elders always ask 'What would the Founder do?' before making big decisions," said Logio. "Perhaps we should ask the same question. What would the Founder do to address this problem? Mr. Philo, you knew the Founder. What do you think he would have done?"

"Give me a minute," responded Mr. Philo as he disappeared into the book stacks. He returned moments later holding a dusty volume (Figure 5). "This is from the Founder's library and has marginal notes in the Founder's own hand. Perhaps this will help you formulate a plan."

"This book belonged to the Founder? Wow!" chorused the friends.

Figure 5 The Founder's book.

Blowing the dust off, the friends could see part of the cover was torn from frequent use. They could only make out part of the title: …*My Cheese*. It was a small book, and on the title page in the Founder's own hand was written "This started me on my journey to found the Community."

Finding a quiet corner, the four friends took turns reading the small volume aloud. When they had finished the story, they looked at each other and vowed, "Now we know what we have to do."

Impatiently, the four friends waited until the date for the next open meeting to arrive. The friends got there early and sat in the first row directly in front of the Elders. The meeting proceeded as usual, and finally the Herald asked, "Are there any questions for the Elders?"

This time there was no hesitation. Visio rose and addressed the Elders. "In the last meeting we shared our data with you about the diminishing cheese supply. We were guilty of providing you with data but no plan, and we apologize for that. However, this time we have a plan. In the Founder's library we found a copy of this book with notes in the Founder's own hand." Visio held up the book for all to see. "The book inspired our plan—we must look for cheese in the maze outside the Community."

There was a collective gasp from all in the room. The Elders looked at each other. After what seemed like a very long time, the CEO broke the silence. "We always ask 'What would the Founder do?' when faced with big decisions. Tell us what the book says that resulted in your proposing such a risky plan."

Visio did not hesitate. "The Founder wrote that this book provided him with the impetus and the courage to venture into the maze. He discovered lots of cheese here and founded the Community. The Founder had the courage to venture into the maze. We too must find the courage that the Founder had and do likewise."

"Do you understand what you are proposing?" asked the CEO. "Over the years several foolhardy members of our Community have ventured into the maze. None has ever returned. That is why we have firmly discouraged such an idea. And now you are asking us to venture into the maze to look for cheese?"

"Not exactly, sir," said Visio. "My friends and I are proposing that the Council give us permission and the resources so that *we* can venture into the maze and look for more cheese."

Producing a large map (Figure 6), Mauri held it up for people to see and said, "This is a copy of the map of the Community at the entrance to the Library. Most people pass by without noticing it, but I always stop to examine it. The map provides the clue to the only place where we might find more cheese." Mauri paused. "Think about it, sir. We all know the Community, and we know that there is no cheese here except the cheese in the Warehouse. But we don't know the maze. We need to look outside of the Community in the maze. We need to check it out to see if there is more cheese in the maze."

The CEO pondered for a moment. "So you four are proposing to venture into the maze to look for more cheese? There could be all sorts of dangers there."

"That is a scary thought, but the most fearsome thing is the unknown," said Cassandra. "We are afraid of the maze because we don't know anything about it. It could be filled with monsters, but it could also be filled with cheese. We need to have the courage to find out."

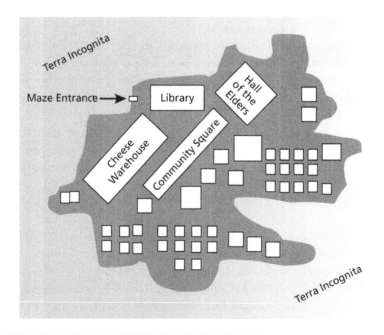

Figure 6 Map of the community.

Logio spoke up for the first time. "What Cassandra says is true. When we deal with the unknown we can either let our imaginations fill us with fear or we can find the confidence to deal with whatever is there. And Mauri is right. We know with certainty where more cheese isn't. We don't know whether there is cheese in the maze, but it is the only place to look."

"Sir," continued Visio, "what we propose is to conduct a small exploration of the maze to see what is there and to begin making a map. I will lead the expedition. Mauri is an excellent map maker, so he will go along. Cassandra has a real skill for anticipating opportunities and threats. She will be our guide. Logio will manage the resources. We believe that we can get a good feel for whether there are opportunities in the maze in about five days. We calculate that we will need about forty pounds of cheese, map-making tools, and some other things. We have a list. We can do this if you will support us. If we find nothing or do not return, what have you lost?"

The CEO surveyed the faces of the Elders. "Give me the book, Mr. Visio. The Council will adjourn for thirty minutes to discuss your proposal."

"All rise. The meeting is temporarily adjourned," intoned the Herald.

The Elders retired to their private meeting chamber. One of the Elders opened the discussion. "They are a bunch of trouble makers. They will stir fears among the Community. We have to shut them up."

"But what if they are right?" asked another Elder.

"We have always had enough cheese. The Founder saw to that," retorted the first Elder.

"But they have put us in a difficult situation by bringing in the Founder's book," the second Elder replied. "If we ignore them, we appear to be ignoring the Founder's teaching. I say we let them go into the maze. If they come back with cheese—great. If they do not come back, their troublemaking will be at an end."

The discussion continued with some seeming to acknowledge that a problem with the cheese supply existed, others denying it, and yet others taking no position on that point at all. Finally a vote was taken.

After what seemed to be many hours, but was in reality just thirty minutes, the Elders returned. "All rise," repeated the Herald.

The CEO remained on his feet. "Everyone please be seated," he began. "Mr. Visio, we have considered your plan and we will support your expedition into the maze. We remind you of the risk that you are taking. If you do return bloody and bowed, there will be no more talk of running out of cheese or venturing into the maze. Agreed?"

"Yes sir. We agree."

"When do you propose to begin?"

"We can be ready by the end of the week. Here is our list of the resources we need. Thank you sir," said Visio, as the Elders stood up to leave.

"All rise!" came the familiar voice of the Herald.

The four friends restrained themselves until the Elders had departed the hall. Then they gave high fives all around.

It takes more than facts to convince decision makers of the need to change.

The most fearsome thing is the unknown.

5

Exploring the Maze—
An Unsettling Discovery

Visio and the exploration team assembled near the entrance to the maze to inventory their resources and to review the exploration plan they had established in previous meetings at the Library. The team was to consist of four members. Visio was the natural choice to be team leader. Logio, Cassandra, and Mauri were selected because they had skills vital to the success of the expedition. Logio was known for his ability to manage resources, Cassandra was known for her critical thinking and forecasting skills, and Mauri was a talented draftsperson and surveyor. All were part of a larger group of friends who regularly met at the Library for freewheeling discussions of a wide range of topics. Other members of the group expressed interest in joining the expedition, but the Elders had allocated only forty pounds of cheese to the team, which was sufficient only for a five-day expedition by the four friends. Additionally, the Elders had specified that the group be small. After all, no one had ever ventured into the maze and returned, so the Elders did not wish to risk too many resources on such a risky expedition.

In addition to the cheese, the group had collected some rope, a logbook, paper for map making, a couple of carts to carry their supplies, candles and lanterns, some chalk to mark their path through the maze, and other assorted equipment. Of course they also carried the Founder's book for moral support.

Visio and his team had determined that the objectives of this expedition were:

- to conduct a limited exploration of the maze;
- to map the maze as they went;

- to identify opportunities and threats that may exist in the maze;

- and, ideally, to return with more cheese than they started with.

Even if they were unable to achieve the last objective, they hoped that merely returning safely would be sufficient to convince the Elders to fund a more extensive exploration of the maze.

Two Elders unlocked the heavy door securing the entrance to the maze and struggled to open it. Bidding goodbye to those gathered to see them off, the team entered the maze. They had taken only a few steps inside the maze when they heard the door close and the lock click into place.

As Logio checked the carts once again, Mauri unfolded the map paper and began documenting their starting point. "Well, here we are, in the maze at last. We're on our own now," said Mauri, trying to sound braver than he was.

The team surveyed their position. There was only one path to take from the door to the maze so off they went. Each time they encountered a fork in the path or a side chamber, Mauri would carefully document it, and they would mark it with a number in chalk so that they could follow the same path back. The rest of the first day was uneventful except for Mauri's constant complaints about how heavy his pack was.

On the second day of moving through the maze, they came to a side path that was secured by an old rotting door. Pushing the door open, they beheld a very large chamber—almost as large as the one containing the Community. But what they saw in the chamber caused them to draw back in fear and astonishment.

Inside the chamber were the dusty ruins of a community. There were crumbling buildings, including one that looked as large as the Cheese Warehouse in their Community. Worse yet, there were the bones of the inhabitants. As they explored deeper into the chamber, they found one particularly disturbing skeleton whose hand still held a few crumbs of moldy cheese. This skeleton wore clothes that were different from the others.

"Those clothes look like the ones we wear!" exclaimed Cassandra. "Do you suppose this person is one of the people who entered the maze long ago and never returned?"

"Who can tell," responded Visio. "Let's finish our exploration of the chamber quickly and get out of here. This is not a good place to be."

The team began exploring the chamber looking for cheese. They found what appeared to be a cheese warehouse, but it was empty. There were remnants of signs on the outside of the warehouse announcing increasingly smaller cheese rations. All in all, it was a very depressing place.

After several hours in the chamber, the only cheese they'd found were the crumbs in the skeleton's hands. So Mauri carefully documented the chamber on the map, and the team gently closed the door as they returned to the maze.

"Whew! That was disturbing," said Logio. "This community obviously did well for a time, then...."

"Then it died!" Cassandra exclaimed. "They ran out of cheese and they all died. That could be us a few years from now if we don't find more cheese. There is no guarantee that the cheese supply will last forever."

"No, that won't happen. It can't. There must be more cheese in the maze. We just have to keep looking," said Visio.

6

Persevering

On the third day of the exploration Logio, who was in charge of resources for the group, again reminded Visio that their cheese supply was running low. "If we don't turn around now, we won't have enough cheese to make it back to The Community."

"Just a little farther. I want to explore this passage. We haven't mapped it yet and we don't know what it might contain." There was a trace of desperation in Visio's voice.

"But we don't have enough cheese to do that, Visio, we must turn back now!" pleaded Logio. Cassandra chimed in, "I agree with Logio. I predict dire consequences if we don't turn back now. No one has ever done what we have done. Let's be satisfied with that. We can just tell the Elders that we didn't find anything that can help us. I don't want to starve in this maze."

Visio knew that he had to say something. "Exploration involves risk. We have to take a chance or our expedition will only prove that someone can enter the maze and return unscathed. That's not enough. We have to find out what is in the maze. We can cut our daily cheese rations a bit and stretch our supply to give us two more days to explore this passage. We've come too far to quit now. Are you with me or not?"

"Okay, I'm with you," responded Logio. After a heated discussion, Mauri agreed to go with Visio too, but Cassandra was not convinced. "I still think this will not turn out well. No one has made it back from the maze. This foolhardy extension of our exploration will seal our fates too. I say we go home now," insisted Cassandra.

Visio started to respond, but Logio beat him to it. "Cassandra, we all are afraid, even Visio, I think. The unknown is bad enough, and to venture further with limited resources is very risky. But he is right. Our goal is to find more cheese, and so far we haven't done that. We have to keep going. The fate of the Community is at stake. Please, come with us."

Cassandra reluctantly agreed. "Very well, but I predict disaster!"

Another day passed as they explored a new passage. Since finding what they had begun to call the "Dead Community," they had found nothing but empty rooms and dead ends. Now they had rounded another bend and had found yet another dead end with a room off to the side. Like most of the rooms they had found, it was empty except for a thick layer of dust.

The explorers' stomachs were growling from the reduced cheese ration. From this point they would have to retrace their steps for the two-hour journey back to the last fork in the maze. Visio was becoming discouraged and thought to himself: "I am responsible for this—another dead end. We were just lucky it was not another dead community. We might not be so lucky next time. Cassandra was right. No one will follow me now." When they arrived at the fork, he turned to the group. "Cassandra was right. It was foolish of me to lead you off into this unknown passage when our resources were running so low. And who knows what dangers might be in the maze? As much as I want to continue the search for more cheese, I just don't have it in me to try another unknown fork in the maze and possibly lead us to our doom. Let's go home."

Cassandra stood up to speak. Visio anticipated the "I told you so" that he felt he richly deserved. "Wait a minute," she said, "I know I was against this extension of our exploration, but I have had time to think about what Visio and Logio said." Turning to Visio, she said, "You were right. We have come too far to quit now. A dead end is just a temporary setback. Besides, we have new information to use to update our map. The map will show others that there is nothing of interest here, so we have accomplished something. We have expanded our knowledge of the maze. And we all knew there was possible danger in the maze, but we have faced one scary situation and are all okay. We have enough resources to spend another two days exploring this fork if we all agree to strict rationing. Who knows what will be around the next corner? Visio, you uncovered the problem, you convinced the Elders to sponsor our expedition. You are our leader. We are ready to follow you to explore this next fork. Right, team?"

A cheer went up. "Yes! Yes! Let's continue on!" they shouted.

Visio's spirits were lifted, but a simple "thank you" was all he could manage for a moment. Then he said "We are a great team not because of me but because of all of us. Without Logio's management of our resources, we couldn't have made it this far. Mauri's maps have kept us from doubling back on our path and will assure that we can find our way home. And Cassandra's predictions have been more true than not. Everyone working together is what makes this a great team. I am proud to be your leader. Let's go!"

After another two hours in the new passage, they encountered yet another room. But this room was different. In the far corner of the room was a small pile of cheese. In total it was probably only four or five times the amount of their original rations. While it was somewhat different from the cheese they were used to, they sniffed it and then they tried it. Everyone agreed it tasted good. In their exuberance, they all feasted until everyone had eaten his or her fill. It was the first time in days that that they had full stomachs, and it felt good.

After the feast they discussed what to do next. Visio proposed, "Let's set aside enough cheese to allow us to explore to the end of this passage and return home. We will package the rest of the cheese to give to the Elders. We should be able to return with at least three times the amount of cheese they allotted for this expedition. This will prove to the Elders that there is good reason to explore the maze."

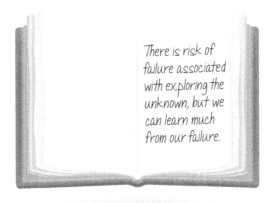

There is risk of failure associated with exploring the unknown, but we can learn much from our failure.

7
The Return Home

It had been two days since the friends' triumphant return to the Community. Everyone was astounded and relieved that they had survived their trip into the maze. A parade was held and speeches were made. Several Elders spoke about their wisdom in conceiving of the plan to explore the maze. "We knew that there would be more cheese in the maze and these explorers have proved it." But most gave Visio and his friends credit for selling the idea to explore the maze, and everyone remarked on their courage. A ceremony was held to place Mauri's map of the maze (Figure 7) next to the map of the Community.

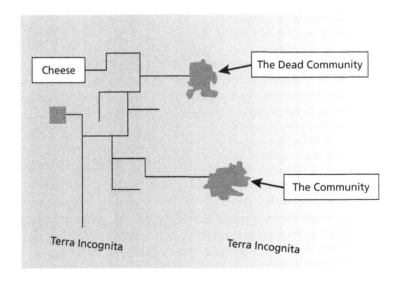

Figure 7 Mauri's map of the maze.

Public tasting parties, hosted by the Elders, were held so that Community members could taste the new cheese. Most were effusive in their praise of the new cheese, but a few complained that its taste and texture were different from the cheese they were accustomed to eating.

Some entrepreneurial-minded members talked about leading guided tour groups through the maze. One even approached Visio to ask him to drop out of the exploration team so that he could make his fortune as a tour guide. The Elders were careful to secure the entrance to the maze and posted a sign forbidding unauthorized entry.

Mauri worked with the engineers in the Bicycle Shop to develop improved surveying and mapping equipment. Orville and Wilber, the Bicycle Shop engineers, were very talented and Mauri had worked with them on many innovative ideas over the years.

Visio and his friends enjoyed the celebrations, but immediately began planning their next step. This time they did not have to wait for an open meeting—the Elders scheduled private meetings to discuss what the team had learned and to determine the prospects for a larger mission to find more cheese.

Many residents clamored to be included in the next expedition. This bothered Visio and his friends a bit. "Where were they when we needed support for the first expedition?" asked Cassandra. Visio answered, "Mr. Philo once told me 'Nothing succeeds like success!'"

But despite these feelings, the friends knew that they needed additional team members for the next expedition, so they began screening the applicants. Eventually they selected four additional members to join them. Two were charged to help Mauri with the mapping of the maze and two to help Logio with logistics. The four new members included Bromo, who had deserted the team early on. He had made a point of apologizing for his actions before the first expedition began and asked to join them. This offer was declined, but Bromo did have skills and a strong back—good for pulling one of the carts Logio planned to use for carrying supplies out and cheese back on the return.

Brutus, another friend who had deserted the team with Bromo, also apologized and made a point of attending the friends' planning meetings. He demurred when asked to be a part of the next expedition, saying he had recently been appointed to a new position by the Elders and could not afford to be away from his new job.

There was no shortage of suggestions from Elders and community members for the next expedition. Visio had to appeal to the CEO for a place where the team could meet in private. "You may use the office next to mine, and I have provided a small budget for you to use to develop your plan," said the CEO. "Be sure to keep me informed of your plans and the schedule for the next expedition. And don't forget, you must present your plan to the Elders before we will allocate resources to support the next expedition."

At last the team was ready to make their presentation to the Elders. "The size and scope of this expedition exceeds that of our initial foray into the maze," said Visio. "We now know well the parts of the maze we previously explored, thanks to Mauri and his maps. Mauri was also careful to mark each branch of the maze with chalk so that we will always know where we are while in the mapped branches. As we explore new branches we will continue to expand the map and mark the branches. We are also carrying more provisions. We will leave caches of supplies along the way for the return home so that we will have more room on the carts for the cheese we hope to find." The Elders adjourned for private discussion, after which they gave the plan their unanimous approval.

The team spent the next several days accumulating their supplies and loading them on the four large carts they were taking with them. This time there would be no rationing as they were allocated as much cheese as they requested. Mauri's surveying and mapping gear was carefully stowed on the first cart.

This time there was a large crowd at the entrance as Visio and the team prepared to enter the maze for their second expedition. After many speeches and much cheering, Visio and the team waved as they entered the maze. The entrance to the maze was secured behind the team with an ominous clank.

8

The Second Expedition

Three days into the expedition and things were going as expected. Still in a section of the maze they had previously explored, Mauri tested his new mapping equipment and worked to improve the accuracy of his map. The team left caches of supplies for their return trip at each spot where they stopped for the night. This reduced their load and made more room on the carts for the cheese they hope to find. So far, they had found only empty chambers, but there were new passages yet to be explored.

A few days later they dropped off the last cache, which meant they had one more day to explore new passages before they would need to turn back. They had found several chambers that contained small amounts of cheese, and they had packaged and loaded the cheese on the carts. The really big store of cheese they hoped for had eluded them. But they were not discouraged, hoping it would be found just around the next corner.

After another day of fruitless searching, they prepared for the return journey. They had two carts full of new cheese that they had only sampled since they had brought plenty of cheese with them. The new cheese seemed to be different in each location, but all of it tasted good.

When they reached the location of their first cache on the return trip, they were surprised to see that it wasn't there! "It must be here," exclaimed Mauri. "It is marked on the map and we marked the location on the wall." The team split up and quickly checked the surrounding areas of the maze for the missing cache of cheese while Mauri remained in place, checking and rechecking his map with the notations documenting the location of the caches.

Cassandra was the first to return. "I found nothing. I have an eerie feeling about this. Could there be others in the maze who took our cheese?"

"All we have found is the Dead Community," Mauri responded. "But that does open the possibility that there are other communities that we just haven't found yet."

Soon all of the remaining members had returned except for Logio. None had found any signs of the cache. Cassandra and Mauri shared their speculation that perhaps there were others in the maze.

"What if they are hostile?" responded Visio. "Should we set up a defense in case they are still nearby?"

Just then they heard Logio shout "Hey! Come look at this. I found footprints leading off into this side passage and crumbs of cheese."

The team ran to join Logio. As they gathered and examined the footprints there was more discussion about what to make of this. Even though they had found evidence that others had been in the maze in the past, this was the first real evidence indicating that others were *still* in the maze. Instinctively the team huddled together as if to draw strength from the others' close presence.

Then Visio had a revelation. "I just thought of something. We know that the Founder came from somewhere in the maze. We have his book and all of the stories Mr. Philo has told us. The Founder was a person just like us. Perhaps we are overreacting to the possible danger associated with the presence of others."

"Yes, but they stole our cache," Bromo said. "That's not a friendly act."

"But we have been taking cheese where we found it too. What if the cheese we have been finding is their cheese? Then we would be seen as thieves," Mauri said.

"Mauri is right," Cassandra said. "We can't just assume that every unknown is evil. We have to be open-minded about things that are new to us."

Visio responded. "I agree with you, Cassandra, but we also must exercise due caution and not just blindly assume the unknown is either good or evil. It is just 'unknown' until we explore it. Let's do this. Bromo, you stay with the carts to be sure no one takes them. The rest of us will follow these footprints to see where they lead us."

With that, everyone but Bromo slowly entered the passage and began following the footprints.

We have to be open-minded about things that are new to us.

9

The Encounter

The team followed the footprints for about fifteen minutes. They moved very slowly. They did not want to surprise whoever made the footprints and they did not want to be surprised by them either. They all put on brave faces, but each harbored thoughts about worst-case scenarios. Visio tried to keep the team focused on the positive possibilities. "This could be a great opportunity. No one from our Community has interacted in any way with someone or something in the maze. We will be the first. Who knows what they know that we can learn from them."

"You are right," Cassandra said. "I know that it is dangerous, but I am excited and I predict that we can learn much once we find whoever made these footprints. We must be careful not to allow our fears to blind us to the potential good that might result from our encounter with the unknown."

Just then Mauri, who was in the lead, stopped abruptly. "Look at this. Whoever made the footprints stopped here. Judging from the signs, it appears there were three individuals. And look here. There are crumbs of our cheese and tiny droplets of a white liquid."

As the team examined these signs, they heard a noise from the chamber just up the passage.

Quietly, the team moved to the entrance to the chamber. Cautiously, they looked into the chamber. There they saw three individuals that looked not too dissimilar from themselves. The three were talking as they unwrapped the cache of cheese they had taken. While their language was somewhat different from that of the Community, it was easily understandable. They were speculating about what the cheese was. It appeared that they were totally unfamiliar with cheese!

The team members withdrew a bit from the chamber entrance and whispered among themselves about what to do next. They finally decided to announce themselves quietly and as non-threateningly as possible.

Visio led the way. He knocked softly and slowly moved into the entrance so that he could be seen. He held his hands high as he said in as friendly and confident a voice as he could muster, "We come in peace."

All three individuals leaped to their feet. Despite Visio's efforts to appear non-threatening, their eyes were wide and they were obviously frightened. "Please don't be afraid. I am here with friends and we mean you no harm." Visio said. "We are from the Community. Who are you and where do you come from?"

The three appeared to relax only slightly. Unlike the friends from the Community, they had not had the benefit of seeing footprints that indicated someone else was in the maze before actually encountering them. So this was a greater shock to them than it was to the friends.

"Please. We would just like to talk. I have others with me," Visio said as he motioned for his friends to show themselves. "That is our cheese you have. We left it in the passageway. We were just trying to find what happened to it. But we have plenty of cheese with us, and we are not angry that you took it. Can we just talk?"

The three individuals exchanged glances and whispered among themselves for a few minutes. Then one of the three stepped forward and spoke. "I am Etude, and these are my teammates, Roswell and Marfa. We are from the Village and are the first to enter the maze. We did not steal this parcel you call cheese. We found it and took it to try to determine what it is. We did not know that it was owned by anyone. We had no idea anyone else was in the maze."

The ensuing discussion was circumspect. Each side was careful not to divulge anything that might be a threat to themselves or the homes they came from. Mauri was careful to conceal his maps. The Villagers were careful not to divulge where the Village was located. Despite this, the talks were friendly and the Villagers even joked about the Community team's strange accents. Then Visio sent Logio to find Bromo and have him join them in the chamber.

The friends explained what cheese was, since the Villagers were unfamiliar with it. They showed them that it was good to eat and prepared samples from the cache for the Villagers to sample. The Villagers found it strange, but good.

They explained that their resource was milk—the white droplets that the friends had found in the passageway. It was distributed within the Village in much the same way as cheese was distributed in the Community. They offered the friends small glasses of milk to sample. The friends found it tasted good.

"I propose that we make an exchange," Visio said. "You take our cache of cheese with you in exchange for a large flask of your milk." The proposal was eagerly accepted with handshakes all around.

"I further propose that we designate this chamber as The Meeting Ground," Visio said, as he chalked the name on the wall of the chamber. He also sketched a box underneath the name. "In this space we can leave messages for each other. Should we desire to meet again, we can exchange messages and agree on a time to meet here." He handed a piece of chalk to Etude, who agreed to the plan.

Logio and Bromo arrived and the two groups spent several more hours discussing many things. Eventually both decided it was time to depart. The Villagers shouldered the caches of cheese and the friends loaded the flask of milk onto one of the carts. They shook hands and exchanged messages of good will as they went their separate ways.

We must be careful not to allow our fears to blind us to the potential good that might result from our encounter with the unknown.

10

We Are Not Alone
in the Maze

Upon their return to the Community the team publicly presented the new cheese to the Elders. As before there was excitement about the new cheese, but this time some expressed disappointment that the team had not found more. After the public celebration of the team's return from the maze, Visio asked the Elders to meet with the team in private session so that he could provide a complete report. He didn't want to make public the presence of the Village without first informing the Elders. He remembered something Mr. Philo had told him a long time ago, "The Elders do not like public surprises."

That afternoon Visio and his friends arrived to meet with the Elders in private. When they arrived Brutus was talking with the CEO. Brutus nodded to the friends, then took a seat at the side of the room.

Visio began by saying, "We are not alone in the maze." The Elders reacted with great surprise. After they calmed down a bit, he recounted the meeting with the party from the Village. The Elders gave him their full attention and asked many questions.

Visio provided small samples of the milk from the Village party that he had traded for. One Elder commented that the milk "wasn't too disagreeable." Another said he liked it. All the Elders expressed great interest in this new material. "I propose we provide the bulk of the milk to the engineers in the Bicycle Shop. They can study its properties to determine whether it might be useful to us."

The Elders endorsed this proposal. The CEO then rose and said with great seriousness, "Until we know everything about this milk, do not tell anyone else about it or the team from the Village. We have much to deliberate about before we are prepared to make a general announcement about these extraordinary discoveries. Have the engineers in the Bicycle Shop pledge that they will also maintain silence about their work."

"All rise!" intoned the Herald.

"Quiet!" shouted the CEO. "This is not an open meeting. For the record, this meeting never happened." With that the Elders and Brutus filed out of the room talking earnestly among themselves. Visio and his friends picked up the flask of milk and headed to the Bicycle Shop. Brutus joined them for the trip.

Two days later the friends were summoned to meet with the Elders. The CEO rose and looked at Visio and his friends. "You have demonstrated that there is new cheese in the maze. So far the quantities have been modest, but you have demonstrated the potential. Your discovery of the others in the maze makes us aware that it is possible that we may have competition for that cheese. We must move rapidly before the others get it all. You have done a magnificent job during your exploration and you will be rewarded with a citation for your work. Now it is time to increase the scale of our work in the maze. Next week Brutus will lead a large-scale expedition into the maze with the objective of finding the large stores of cheese that must exist there."

Visio was stunned. "Sir, do you mean that Brutus will lead us on the next expedition?"

"No," replied the CEO. "Brutus has hand-picked a team of professionals that he will lead into the maze. Your work is complete."

"But what about the milk?" asked Visio.

"The milk is an interesting substance, but what we need is cheese," replied the CEO. "You may continue your work examining the milk as you wish. Please keep Brutus in the information loop. He will inform us of your results."

With that, the meeting was ended and Visio and his friends were dismissed. They looked at each other in disbelief. They were speechless. Brutus stopped for a moment before joining the Elders. "Nice work, guys. Now we experts will take this project to the next level."

They glared at Brutus as he left to join the Elders. Finally Cassandra whispered, "People aren't always as they seem."

"Yes," replied Visio. "I thought Brutus was with us. He just wanted the information we had so that he could curry favor with the Elders. Now he has a special place with the Elders and we have been dismissed."

"That snake!" exclaimed Mauri.

There was nothing else to do, so Visio and his friends slowly left the meeting room. Visio suggested they visit Mr. Philo tomorrow at the Library for advice. Everyone agreed.

"I must run," exclaimed Visio suddenly. "I have a dance class in just ten minutes. I was late for my last class, and the instructor scolded me."

"Dance class! Since when did you study dance?" asked Cassandra.

"Mr. Philo advised that I would benefit from engaging in a diverse set of experiences," replied Visio. "I have always appreciated dance, but have never tried it. Besides, it should help me become stronger and more agile."

The next day the friends met at the Library as planned. Mr. Philo listened silently as the friends related what happened in the meeting with the Elders and their betrayal by Brutus. When they were finished, Mr. Philo asked, "What do you plan to do now?"

"What can we do?" asked Cassandra. "We're out and Brutus is in. There will be no more exploring of the maze by us."

"Yeah! I think we should just put all of this behind us and get on with what we have always done," Mauri added.

Obviously, emotions were high. Mr. Philo listened to the friends venting their emotions. When the outbursts of emotion finally ended, the friends just sat there with their heads down.

"Well," began Mr. Philo, "I think you have but two choices: quit or persevere. You need to let go of your emotional response and think about this more rationally. Is the problem you have been addressing real and important?"

"Yes! Of course," responded Visio. "If we run out of cheese, we will become like the Dead Community."

"Okay. If the problem is real and important, you must persevere in spite of setbacks in order to solve it. So the next question is, what else can you do to help solve the problem?" continued Mr. Philo.

"We could work with the engineers at the Bicycle Shop to find new uses for the milk," Mauri said.

"Yes, and perhaps we could also help develop a plan for establishing a relationship with the Villagers. They may have some ideas we haven't thought of that might help solve our problem," Logio added.

"Then why are you sitting here with your heads down?" Mr. Philo asked. "Get a move on. Off to the Bicycle Shop. Let me know what you discover about the milk."

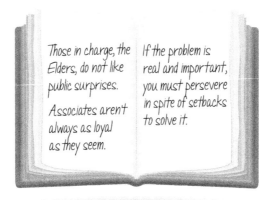

Those in charge, the Elders, do not like public surprises.

Associates aren't always as loyal as they seem.

If the problem is real and important, you must persevere in spite of setbacks to solve it.

11

The Debacle
and the Opportunity

Brutus and his team entered the maze the following week. The team consisted of twenty people with ten large carts, an indication of the amount of cheese they hoped to bring back to the Community. Visio had offered his advice and Mauri had offered his maps, but Brutus waved them away. "We have sufficient resources to handle this on our own," he said.

Three weeks passed, and the friends and the Bicycle Shop engineers had made some interesting findings about the milk, but they still had much more work to do before they completed their analysis. It was at this time that a message was received from the Elders, inviting Visio and his friends to meet with them that afternoon.

When the friends arrived, they were escorted into the private chambers of the Elders. "Before we begin, we must charge you with maintaining the utmost secrecy concerning what we are about to discuss."

The friends nodded their agreement with the charge.

The CEO began. "Last night Brutus returned from the maze—alone! It seems that the expedition had found no cheese and feared they were lost. Then they heard the sound of a monster in the maze and panic ensued. Brutus said that it was every man for himself in getting home. He abandoned the team and somehow found his way back to the Community. But there are still nineteen team members who have not returned and Brutus refuses to reenter the maze. We need you to find the remaining team members and bring them home. Will you accept this task?"

After a brief discussion among themselves, Visio spoke for the team. "Certainly we will do all that we can to find the team members and guide them home. But we have a special request to make."

"We will hear your request," the CEO said.

"We have made an astounding finding about the milk. We have been working with the engineers in the Bicycle Shop to characterize the milk and to determine what it might be good for. We have found that you can make cheese from the milk!"

The Elders looked at each other, but it was obvious that they did not understand the importance of this finding.

Visio continued. "The Villagers told us they had a virtually unlimited supply of milk. If we could convince them to share the milk with us, then we could have an unlimited supply of cheese. Do you see? This could solve our cheese supply problem."

"And what do you suppose the Villagers would want in return?" the CEO asked.

Cassandra responded, "We believe the Villagers would be willing to give us milk if we agreed to provide them with some of the cheese we make from it. They seemed to like the cheese that we gave them. It would be a win-win situation for both us and them."

Mauri interjected, "We would like to invite the leaders of the Village to send representatives to meet with representatives you designate. The meeting would take place in the chamber where we first met them. We would also like to leave them a bundle of cheese as a show of good faith."

The Elders talked briefly among themselves. "We see considerable risk in what you propose. We must deliberate before giving you an answer. We will do so while you secretly gather the provisions you need for the rescue mission. We will have an answer for you before you depart."

With another stern warning about the need to maintain absolute secrecy about the upcoming mission, the friends were dismissed.

Debacles can sometimes be sources of opportunities.

12

The Elder's Debate

While the friends prepared for their secret mission, the Elders debated among themselves about what their answer should be to the friends' proposal.

Although most of the Elders were favorably disposed, a small group voiced its concerns about the proposed alliance with the other community. "This proposal to trade our cheese for milk is too risky. How do we know that we can trust the other community? Our cheese supply is already declining. It is foolhardy to give away our cheese not knowing whether we can trust them to provide us with milk."

Kindunos, another of the Elders, responded. "You raise a good point, but rather than forgoing this opportunity to assure our cheese supply through an alliance with the other community, let's work to minimize those risks. After all, the Founder was not averse to risk, but he did take care to manage that risk. As I see it, we are faced with two choices: (1) Do nothing and risk running out of cheese or (2) take a calculated risk to form an alliance with the other community that can benefit both of us. The former minimizes the short-term risk associated with sharing information but does nothing to minimize the long-term risk of running out of cheese. Properly structured, the latter can minimize both the short-term and long-term risks. A successful alliance can increase the diversity and supply of resources for both communities."

The others had a quick rejoinder. "Well, what if the other community steals our technology and decides to make their own cheese? Where are we then?"

"We must enter into this relationship in the right way," Kindunos replied. "We must get to know the leaders of the other community and establish an atmosphere of trust. And we must make the very best quality cheese so that they have no incentive to try to make their own. After all, we have developed the cheese-making technology. Who is in a position to make better cheese than we are?"

More discussion ensued, but in the end the Elders voted to accept the proposal to meet with representatives of the other community. They formed a committee tasked with preparing for the first meeting. The job of the committee was to assess whether forming a mutually beneficial alliance with the Village was feasible. The Elders were careful to include on the committee members of the group who expressed reluctance to form the alliance, and the Elders voted to include Visio on the committee. This was the first time that an ordinary Community member had ever been included on a committee of Elders.

"Of course, before we actually conclude an agreement we must visit the other community to meet with its governing body in order to assess its capabilities to fulfill its end of the agreement and to determine whether their residents are trustworthy," said Kindunos, the Elder who was selected to chair the committee. "This will be just an initial meeting."

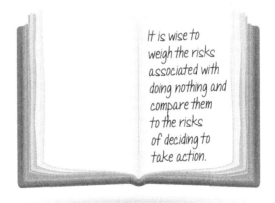

It is wise to weigh the risks associated with doing nothing and compare them to the risks of deciding to take action.

13

The Rescue Mission

Fully provisioned and with the Elders' permission to arrange a meeting with the other community, the friends entered the maze in the dead of night so that they would not be seen. "The Elders are sensitive about choosing Brutus over you to lead the second expedition. They are afraid of how the Community members will react to their poor decision," Cassandra reminded Visio. Mauri's map and the markings they had made at intersections in the maze enabled them to navigate confidently to the Meeting Ground where they left a note from the Elders and a small bundle of cheese.

The continued their journey through the maze, mapping the new areas as they went and marking all intersections so that they could easily find their way home once they found the missing expedition members.

On their fifth day in the maze, in a passage they had not been in previously, they found the missing members of Brutus's team. Although hungry, they were in good spirits now that they saw they had been rescued. Logio immediately broke out a package of cheese and they all sat down to eat their fill. While they were eating, Cassandra asked the rescued team to talk about their ordeal.

"Well, it wasn't good from the start. Brutus was a timid leader. He was always hearing things and holding us back. He tried to get us to turn around after the second night, but we refused. We felt we had to come back with cheese. Finally, the next night he wasn't with us. We continued on for several more days finding nothing. Then when we began running low on supplies, we tried to return to the Community. But we were hopelessly lost. Thank goodness you found us."

Mauri quickly guided the explorers home, and they carefully waited until nightfall to emerge from the maze. Mauri used this extra time to update his map of the maze (see Figure 8). The members of Brutus's team headed directly to the Elders to make their report. Visio and his friends decided to wait until the next day to see the Elders, and they retired to their homes.

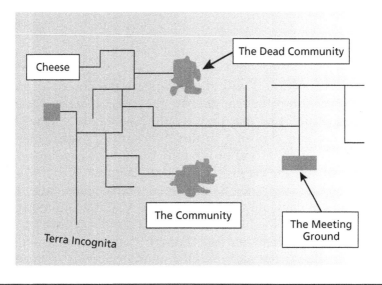

Figure 8 Mauri's updated map of the maze.

14

The Maze Changes

More than a year had passed since the Community and the Village initiated their partnership. Both communities were happy with the arrangement. Brutus only showed himself to receive his weekly cheese rations. He no longer met with the Elders.

During the previous year the Community had blossomed with creative ideas. The Elders encouraged these activities by providing grants and other resources to fund new research into a variety of fields. The Elders initiated an idea program open to everyone in both the Community and the Village. Those who submitted ideas were rewarded with small gifts. Those whose ideas were accepted were acclaimed and given the opportunity to help bring their ideas to fruition. There was much excitement about the program.

Visio was now a key member of the Committee that oversaw the partnership with the Village. In this capacity, he had arranged a visit to the Village by several of the Elders, two of the Bicycle Shop engineers, and several other key members of the Community. Most meetings took place in the chamber where the teams from the two communities first met, which was now known as the Confederation Chamber. The communities also took turns hosting a high-level joint meeting at their location. This time it was the Elders' turn to journey to the Village.

In addition to the necessary provisions for the journey, the visit team was taking along bundles of new cheeses that the Bicycle Shop engineers had developed. One of these was a new experimental soft cheese that the engineers call "Brie." The Villagers had actually proposed the idea of developing a soft cheese because some in their village had difficulty eating the hard cheese that was the Community's staple.

They also took along samples of an entirely new cheese tentatively called "Bleu," part of a cheese batch that had turned out badly. It had an unusual and initially distasteful smell. The engineers had put it aside for more study to determine just what had gone wrong. This caused a potential disruption in scheduled shipments of cheese to the Village. The Elders quickly decided to use cheese from the Cheese Warehouse to fulfil their obligation to the Village. Now the pressure was on to increase cheese production to make up the shortage.

When the engineers finally got around to analyzing the bad batch, they found the cheese rounds to be laced with blue streaks. They determined that this had been caused by some sort of mold that had been introduced during the manufacturing process. When they finished their analysis, the discussion turned to ways of disposing of the bad cheese. One of the engineers suggested that they really should taste a sample to complete their documentation. They drew straws, and one engineer was selected to taste the Bleu cheese. At first the guinea pig made the most horrible expression. But this quickly changed. "It's not as bad as I imagined," he said. They waited a few hours to see whether there were any bad effects from the ingestion of the bad cheese. When there were none, all of them tried a sample. Some liked it, while others hated it. In the end they agreed to hold on to the batch while they had others try samples to see whether there might be some value to this Bleu cheese.

There was little fanfare as the visit team entered the maze. Venturing into the maze was old hat now. There were even day-long tours offered by entrepreneurs who used Mauri's maps to guide them. Still, on ventures that were this important, Mauri and Visio always led the way. Cassandra had joined them this time.

The trip through the maze to the Village took four days. On the third day of the trek, they rounded a corner in the maze and encountered a dead end. "Wait! This can't be," exclaimed Mauri. "This should be a clear passage. This wall wasn't here when we were in the maze previously."

"You must be wrong," Visio said. "This is obviously a solid wall. Your map must be wrong."

"There is nothing wrong with my map. Look at the mark on the wall. It coincides with this point on the map, and the map shows a clear passage," Mauri responded.

"Well, how then do you explain this wall?" Bromo asked.

Without waiting for an answer from Mauri, Cassandra blurted, "The maze changes!"

Visio calmly said, "We can deal with this. It just means that we will have to make more frequent forays into the maze to be sure that our map is always up to date. Meanwhile, we have to find a way to reach the Village."

"This is the only way to reach the Village," said Cassandra. "If we can't reach the Village there will be no milk and no cheese."

"Relax, Cassandra. Give me a few minutes to study the map to try to find an alternate route," said Mauri.

Visio had an insight: "What if we stack several of the carts to form a tower? Perhaps we would be high enough to see over the wall so that we can plot our next move. My dance class has increased my strength and agility, so I am sure I can climb to the top of the tower. C'mon, and give me a hand with this cart."

"Yes! You're a lot stronger and more agile since you have been taking dance lessons. You should easily be able to climb up a tower. Let's get started," said Bromo.

The friends were instantly at work to overcome this latest problem.

Epilogue

If Visio had recorded an entry in his diary later that day, it might have looked like this:

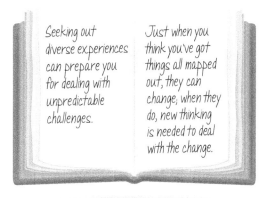

Seeking out diverse experiences can prepare you for dealing with unpredictable challenges.

Just when you think you've got things all mapped out, they can change; when they do, new thinking is needed to deal with the change.

In this Epilogue we will expand on the concepts that are exemplified in the fable. First, we will present a perspective on organizational change. Next, we will consider characteristics of the insightful individual and the insightful organization that make them more likely to come up with breakthrough innovations. Then, after expanding on the content of Visio's diary entries, we will conclude by addressing the relevance of the fable and the takeaways it suggests.

THEORIES OF ORGANIZATIONAL CHANGE

So, why do you think that Visio and his friends had so much trouble convincing the leadership of the Community that a real problem existed and that they had a good idea of how to solve the problem? After all, the facts were there. Who could argue that the cheese was running out? Is this a contrived situation that only exists in our little fictional community? Our research and experience say otherwise. We see situations like this all too often in real organizations of all types including manufacturing, service, healthcare, not-for-profit, educational, and governmental. We see frustrated Visios, dismissive CEOs, unrecognized problems and opportunities, extreme risk-averseness, and all of the other characters and situations in our fable all too often in the real world. Look around you. Do you see them as well? On balance, we have to say that we also see productive teams working in supportive environments accomplishing great things in organizations that are open to new ideas. But our fable is about those organizations that have not yet gotten this right.

Past research helps explain why situations and behaviors such as those in our fable exist. Physics tells us that objects at rest tend to stay at rest unless some force is exerted on them. That force must overcome the inertia of the object. The more massive the object, the more force must be exerted to move it. Organizations are a bit like objects in this way. Unless some force is applied, organizations will tend to continue business as usual. The stronger and more risk-averse the organizational culture that supports the status quo, the more force must be exerted to overcome the "organizational inertia." Of course there are many examples of organizations that embrace risk and encourage change, in which organizational inertia is quite low. Is it possible to make your organization more like those? The answer is yes. Visio and his team helped the Community move from the former to the latter type of organization. But it wasn't easy. Let's examine some change management theories so that we can make sense of situations such as those Visio encountered.

Kurt Lewin provides two models that help explain why change is so difficult to achieve and how we might go about undertaking the process of overcoming those difficulties. The first of the models is known as the Three-Phase Change Model or the Planned Change Model[8] and is depicted in Figure 9.

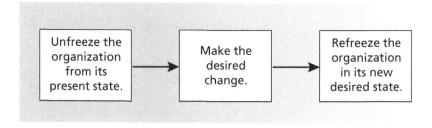

Figure 9 Lewin's Three-Phase Change Model.

The Planned Change Model appears conceptually simple; however, employing the model is anything but simple. "Frozen" is a good term to apply to the present state. The organization arrived at its present state over time and organizational members have become comfortable with that state; they must be provided with convincing motivation to unfreeze. After all, even if the present state is not achieving the results it used to, most people are more comfortable with "the devil we know rather than the devil we don't know." We encounter considerable organizational inertia when trying to change that state.

If the organization successfully unfreezes, making the change is often the easiest phase of the model to accomplish. Once we have unfrozen, a vacuum is created that must be filled. Even if reluctantly, the organization will seek to fill that vacuum with the new desired state.

Refreezing sometimes is as difficult as unfreezing. Often, if insufficient attention is paid to the refreezing step, the organization will backslide into its previous state before the change can take hold. "Holding the gains" of the change process must receive considerable, ongoing attention in order for the organization to be truly transformed. This can be facilitated by establishing an environment where as much of the organization as possible feels that they are part of the change process, that they have had a hand in the project or at least have been seriously listened to. The more people who feel that this is "their change," the easier it will be to gain acceptance for the "new way of doing business." And the change must really be the new way of doing business, consistent with the new culture—not just some add-on to the old culture. It is easier for some who are resistant to change to just ride out an add-on that will run its course and then be forgotten than it is to buy in to a new way of doing things and a new culture.

The second Lewin model is the Force-Field Theory of Change,[9] depicted in Figure 10. This is a complementary model to the Three-Phase Model and indeed provides guidance for facilitating that model of the change process.

The resistance to change is organizational inertia in all of its forms. When the organization is static, there is considerable resistance to change that must be overcome by forces for change. In order to create change, the change agent must either increase the forces for change or decrease the resistance to change or, preferably, do both. Now let's put Lewin's two models together.

In our fable, Visio is desperately trying to unfreeze the Community from its present state, which is doomed to fail, and change it to a desired state that is sustainable long term. He encounters seemingly insurmountable resistance to even acknowledge that a problem exists. What are the sources of the resistance to change? It is easy to blame the CEO or the Elders. But the real resistance to change comes from the organizational culture. The CEO and the Elders see themselves as "the keepers of the culture created by the Founder." They ask, "What would the Founder do?" whenever they are faced with a problem. In a sense they are predestined to resist change that is contrary to the culture they are

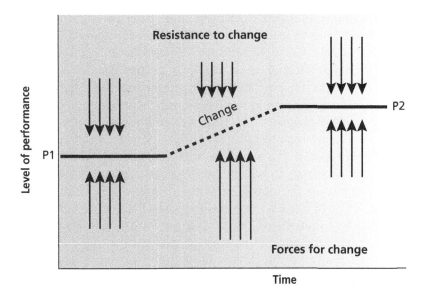

Figure 10 Lewin's Force-Field Theory of Change.

SOURCE: Lewin, *Field Theory in Social Science*

defending. The effect of the organizational culture even extends to individuals lower in the hierarchy—indeed to everyone in the Community. Recall that in our fable, Visio's group of friends decreased from seven to four when Bromo and two others distanced themselves from the group as soon as the group began planning to approach the Elders in the open meeting. That was just too risky for them and they wanted no part of it. Individuals operating in a culture that has a low tolerance for risk are also more likely to be risk-averse. This can make it difficult to recruit colleagues to join a team that might be seen as "bucking the system" in some way.

How did Visio overcome this organizational inertia? He formed a team that was committed to change, which increased the force for change, but since none of the team had any positional power or influence, it was like recruiting additional ants to push against an elephant (Figure 11). This analogy is by no means a disparagement of the power of a team over an individual, nor does it underestimate the effect that a single, highly motivated individual can have on an organization. Indeed, a diverse team with the right kind of leader who is open to the full participation of all group members can bring a variety of perspectives to a project and propose and vet a wider array of ideas. And, as the fable illustrates, team members can be a source of encouragement and strength to each other when the going gets tough. Additionally, having a team rather than an individual propose a course of action can increase the power of the proposal; having one or more members with a track record of success enhances the probability that the team's proposal will be seriously considered. But the power of a team over an individual by itself is seldom sufficient to overcome significant cultural resistance to change.

Visio tried to reduce resistance to change by gathering and using data that proved that change was needed. But, as Visio recorded in his fourth diary entry, this had about the same effect as giving the elephant a haircut to reduce its weight. The effect is tangible, but not sufficient to overcome the resistance to change. Deming used a quote from another source to make this point when he talked about the power of data: *In God we trust. All others must bring data.* Deming implies that many decision makers will not take new ideas seriously if they are not supported by data. So, certainly the probability of success in selling an idea for change is enhanced by having data. But, as with giving the elephant a haircut to reduce its weight, the effect, while tangible, is often not sufficient.

Figure 11 It is difficult to assemble enough ants to move an elephant.

It wasn't until Mr. Philo gave him the Founder's book that Visio began to have success. The book provided the weight of the Founder's words to that of Visio's team, thus increasing the force for change. It added sufficient additional power to enable Visio's small group of ants to have a chance to move the elephant. In addition, it provided Visio a way to present his argument so that it was consistent with the organization's culture, not contrary to it, thus decreasing the forces resisting change. Simultaneously increasing the forces for change while diminishing resistance to change provides a very powerful approach for change agents. Visio further increased his chances of success by proposing an exploratory expedition where the only real risk was borne by his team. Because the resources he needed were small and the proposed expedition was seen as consistent with the Community's culture thanks to the Founder's book, when the CEO and the Elders asked "What would the Founder do?" the answer came from the book and they could hardly say no.

It can be useful early in a project to make two lists: one identifying the forces for change, the other identifying the forces likely to be resistant to change. This is best done as a team exercise, for indeed two, three, or four heads are better than one. A team effort is more likely to develop lists that include the one or two key forces.

It is also helpful to make the list as granular as possible. "Culture" is a big concept comprising many attributes, and thus it is difficult to get your arms around it all at once. Instead of simply listing "organizational culture" as a force resisting change, list the attributes of that culture that resist change. Analyzing the forces resisting change in this way often reveals some of the ways in which these forces can be minimized. For example, one aspect of the Community's culture that resisted change was extreme risk aversion. Visio and his team were able to address this by proposing a plan of action where the team took all of the risk in the first expedition. Indeed if the team failed to return from the maze, the Elders rationalized that this would reinforce their current culture's risk-averseness as well as remove the source of their current discomfort—Visio and his team. So, whether the team's expedition was a success or failure, the Elders were covered. Visio had crafted a proposal where all risks to the Elders had been removed, thus overcoming this point of resistance.

Referring to these lists can be helpful when planning the strategy for presenting proposals to decision makers—the proposals take greatest advantage of the forces for change and proactively anticipate likely resistance to changes being proposed. We invite you to try your hand at this process by completing Exercise 1.

Exercise 1

Use the following blank form to list the forces for change and the forces against change that Visio and his team encountered. As you list them, think about how the characters in the fable addressed each—strengthening the forces for change and weakening the forces against change.

Forces for Change	Forces Resisting Change
1.	1.
2.	2.
3.	3.
4.	4.
5.	5.
6.	6.
7.	7.
8.	8.
9.	9.
10.	10.

After completing the two lists and planning your strategy for dealing with the forces identified in the lists, it is sometimes helpful to role play likely questions and reactions that might occur in the actual meeting. Assign individuals to play the roles of key decision makers who will be in the meeting. Have them view the proposal through the lenses these individuals will use and raise questions that they might raise. Then the presenter(s) can respond to those questions. With others providing feedback and suggestions, these answers can be refined. What was initially an answer of "I don't know" or "I haven't really thought about that" becomes a reasoned response. It is impossible to anticipate all of the questions that might be asked, but this process provides practice for dealing with difficult questions—and that can be the difference between a decision to accept the proposal or to reject it.

Being a change agent like Visio is fraught with risk. In our fable, had Mr. Philo not provided the book, Visio and his team might have been branded as trouble-makers and lost whatever position and influence they had. Once they had obtained permission to go on the exploratory expedition, they might, like those who preceded them into the maze, have never returned. Who knows, there could have been dragons and ogres in the maze and they might have died. And if they had returned safely but with empty hands, they might have been accused of wasting the community's resources and possibly ostracized as foolish, but brave, dreamers whose thoughts and dreams had no practical impact on the organization. Change agents must be courageous as well as resourceful and persistent if real change is to occur.

So, let's review what the fable teaches those who aspire to be agents for change. We will do that by reviewing the lessons the fable teaches and Visio's diary entries, which document the important points he learned from his journey through the change process and how that new knowledge and experience put him on track to becoming an insightful individual and the Community on track to becoming an insightful organization.

THE INSIGHTFUL INDIVIDUAL AND THE INSIGHTFUL ORGANIZATION

Spencer Johnson's original tale *(Who Moved My Cheese?)* succeeded beautifully in challenging the great majority of its readers to accept that fact that change happens—my cheese has been moved!—and to react to that change with a courageous response, rather than head-in-the-sand denial. We certainly believe that courage is needed, but we also believe it is not enough. What is needed is for individuals and organizations to become insightful. What we hoped to dramatize with our fable is how meeting the challenge of change requires not just the actions of isolated individuals, but also putting teams and organizations on the right path. That path is one of increasingly insightful activity. In the process individuals transform themselves, and they transform the larger group—the Community—of which they are a part.

We conceive of insight as "the ability to see reality clearly enough to come up with new ideas that are worth testing."[10] See if you can recognize in the adventures of Visio and his friends several of these characteristics that help develop the capacity for insight:

1. Associate with leaders in the field

2. Acquire the necessary expertise

3. Have a passionate motivation to "see deeply" into a subject

4. Seek out diverse experiences—including those that do not seem directly relevant to what you are studying

5. Be willing to test your ideas (and to let them fail)

6. Let information linger in your memory, in both your conscious and unconscious mind, so that new, fruitful, unexpected connections can be made[11]

In our fable, the actions of Visio and his friends help the Community transform itself so that it is able to test its ideas and run the risk of failing. Because of Visio and his friends, the Community is able to put aside denial and to recognize a serious threat. Bit by bit, the Community comes to recognize the necessity of interacting with the larger world if it is to survive, and the Elders, who were once so hidebound, learn to appreciate the value of exploration and innovation in ways they simply could not have at the beginning. And they gain the self-confidence not to feel threatened when others present them with new ideas.

Visio and his friends also have gained an understanding that in order to be successful innovators, they must possess not only technological skills, but political and facilitation skills as well.[12] Innovative ideas do not become innovations through rational processes alone. What is required is a systems focus and a mastery of all the skills necessary. It is not often that a single person possesses all of the required skills. This is why a team approach is often more successful than trying to go it alone.

As we leave our story, the Community has come to possess a number of the characteristics associated with insightful organizations—those organizations such as 3M and Apple that are "serial innovators." The Community has developed courageous, insightful leadership, has shown an increasing tolerance for risky exploration, encourages the development of its members by funding innovation, is open to ideas from a variety of sources, does not judge ideas too quickly, and sees failure as an opportunity to learn. Thus, by the end of the story the Community has taken great strides forward from the beginning when the Elders' first response to Visio's presentation of the problem is rejection and denial. Now the Community is better positioned to respond with agility to new challenges that will inevitably present themselves.

THE RELEVANCE OF THE FABLE: RECOGNIZING THE NEED TO CREATE NEW CHEESE

One might ask how the Elders in our fable could be so oblivious to the obvious—the cheese is running out. This seems so contrary to the way modern businesses should operate. But a scan of current business headlines is sufficient to dispel the thought that this is just a fable—pure fiction with no possible relevance to the current state of business.

Kodak's cheese supply (emulsion photography) lasted about 100 years. They even developed a new kind of cheese—digital photography—but failed to recognize it as the solution to a problem that they didn't recognize. Others used Kodak's invention to create new cheese, which consumers preferred to Kodak's old cheese. Kodak was too late in trying to obtain some of the new cheese. The result? Bankruptcy and Kodak's trying to find new cheese in their post-bankruptcy reincarnation.

Believe it or not, Kodak is one of the good stories. They have emerged from bankruptcy. Others have not been so fortunate. Borders Bookstores' cheese lasted not nearly so long as Kodak's. The new cheese it helped invent (big-box bookstores) depleted the old cheese of the "mom and pop" bookstores. They and other big-box bookstores dominated the market for reading material for a number of years. Who knew their market better than they? How did they allow new entrants, such as Amazon.com, to deplete their cheese supply? How could they not see that their cheese supply was diminishing? Borders, like Kodak, also were too late in trying to obtain some of the new cheese. Borders declared bankruptcy, closed all of its stores, and no longer exists.

More recently, Blockbuster closed all of its stores. For years, if you wanted to watch a movie at home, you rented a VHS or DVD from Blockbuster. It had what seemed to be an unending supply of cheese. How did Blockbuster not see the rising threat to their cheese of Netflix and others that deliver movies and other content on demand with no need to rewind before returning?

And, after less than a year, Barnes & Noble fired the CEO in August 2016 saying "he wasn't the right person to revamp a bookstore chain struggling to compete with Amazon.com, Inc.... The departure brings fresh upheaval to a chain reeling from the rise of e-books and online rivals."[13] It wasn't that long ago that Barnes & Noble was among those pioneering the new big-box bookstore paradigm that put great pressure on the "mom and pop" bookstores, putting many of them out of business. How is it possible for a company that created its own new cheese to be so blind to the even newer cheese that others were creating? Instead of helping to create this newer cheese, they are struggling to determine how they can obtain some of it before it is too late.

Dell Computer was a relatively early entrant into the PC market. Starting in a University of Texas dormitory room, Michael Dell grew his cheese until at one point Dell was the world's top PC manufacturer. But Dell, too, failed to recognize that its cheese supply was dwindling as integrated devices began decreasing demand for desktop and laptop PCs. Dell has now become a privately owned corporation ostensibly to begin crafting its new incarnation away from the intrusion of Wall Street analysts and shareholders.

These once highly successful firms apparently were lacking a factor that Marcus Wallenberg, chairman of SEB (Skandinaviska Enskilda Banken), has identified as a crucial contributor to a firm's longevity. Here is how he puts it:

> *Joseph Schumpeter (an Austrian economist) focused his attention largely on new businesses and their role in eating the breakfast of established companies. But in my view, "intrapreneurs" — risk takers on the inside — are just as important as entrepreneurs in promoting new ideas and new technology.*[14]

So Visio and his friends are the first generation of "intrapreneurs" in the Community, but, with the evolution of the attitudes of the Elders, we expect that they will not be the last.

THE DIARY ENTRIES—IMPORTANT POINTS

In our fable Visio made diary entries of important points he learned as he went through his adventure. In this section we examine those points. Table 1 contains a list of those points.

Table 1 Visio's diary entries.

---

1. Sometimes you find important things when you aren't looking for them.
2. Simply pointing out a problem is unlikely to result in action.
3. If you propose a radical new idea, don't be surprised if some of your colleagues do not back you.
4. It takes more than facts and a plan to convince decision makers of the need to change.
5. The most fearsome thing is the unknown.
6. There is risk of failure associated with exploring the unknown, but we can learn much from our failure.
7. We have to be open-minded about things that are new to us.
8. We must be careful not to allow our fears to blind us to the potential good that might result from our encounter with the unknown.
9. Those in charge do not like public surprises.
10. Associates aren't always as loyal as they seem.
11. Debacles can sometimes be sources of opportunities.
12. It is wise to weigh the risks associated with doing nothing and compare them to the risks of deciding to take action.
13. Seeking out diverse experiences can prepare you for dealing with unpredictable challenges
14. Just when you think you've got things all mapped out, they can change; when they do, new thinking is needed to deal with the change.

Visio's first diary entry reflects his serendipitously becoming aware of the problem of the diminishing cheese supply. *Serendipity* is a concept first introduced by Horace Walpole[15] in a letter in 1754. Walpole had read a tale in which three princes from Serendip "were always making discoveries, by accident and sagacity, of things which they were not in quest of." So serendipitous discoveries are the result of chance and not the result of a plan—but they are not purely chance! The "sagacity" in Walpole's statement reminds us of Louis Pasteur's saying that "In the fields of observation, chance favors only the prepared mind."

There are two parts to Pasteur's thought. One is that this is a matter of observation. If you remember, in the story Visio found himself in a novel position from which to view the inside of the Cheese Warehouse. The moral of the episode is that, if you want to see things afresh, you may need to change your vantage point. Thus, the CEO who works in disguise as a regular employee and so perceives her organization in a new way is a character we can all appreciate, even if we don't often go to such an extreme.

The second part of Pasteur's thought is that chance favors a prepared mind. Our fable illustrates two aspects to this preparation. First, Visio was made uneasy by the empty expanse of warehouse that he happened to see. Presumably, he was made uneasy by a discrepancy between what he expected to see and what he actually saw. This means that he had a mental model of the situation—one he had probably not given much conscious thought to—a reassuring model of a warehouse comfortably full of cheese. If you have no mental models of a situation, then what happens in a situation cannot strike you as discrepant; it's all just a buzzin', bloomin' confusion.

What happens next is crucial. After Visio noticed the discrepancy, he did not just toss it aside to be forgotten. With the help of his friends, Visio had the drive and the courage to explore the situation further. He wanted to understand what he had seen and what exactly were the implications of that empty expanse of warehouse. Consider Alexander Fleming. When Fleming came back from vacation on a fateful day in September 1928, he observed something unusual in one of the Petri dishes in which colonies of *Staphylococcus* bacteria were growing. The dish was dotted with colonies except for one clear area around a bit of mold. Fleming could have dismissed this as a curiosity, but instead he and his assistants began a series of investigations on the "mould juice" that ultimately put the world on the path to life-saving antibiotics.

So, to summarize, if you want to give serendipity a chance to work for you:

- Even though you aren't looking for those important things to be found by serendipity, you can make it a habit to be observant by actively scanning your environment, occasionally from new vantage points.

- Furthermore, you can put a positive value on the experience of detecting discrepancies between your mental models and observed reality.

- Finally, you can be prepared to put time and other resources to work understanding those discrepancies.

Doing these things increases the odds that you can experience serendipity just as Visio did.

Visio was shocked to discover, as his second diary entry documents, that simply pointing out a problem is unlikely to result in action. It is a human tendency, albeit a bit naïve, to think that something that is clear to you will be equally clear to others. However, we all see the same thing through different lenses or filters and we all have a concept of what "logical" means. The information Visio first brought to the Elders, which through his lens clearly showed that a problem existed, was not perceived by the Elders who viewed it through the cultural lens of the organization. "We have always had enough cheese," and "the Founder provided all of the cheese we need" are the lenses the Elders used. Visio's message was illogical when viewed through the Elders' lenses.

As Visio's third diary entry records, it wasn't just the Elders who failed to see the logic of his interpretation of his observation. Three of Visio's friends abandoned him when what they saw through their lenses was far more risky than what they were prepared to be part of. Their logic differed from Visio's. When proposing a radical new idea, don't be surprised if some of your colleagues do not back you. They see the same things you see, but through different lenses.

Visio and his friends were on the right track when they collected data to support their proposal. But, as Visio's fourth diary entry and our discussion of giving the elephant a haircut show, although data are essential to a proposal for change, data are seldom sufficient to motivate an organization with a strong risk-averse culture to undertake fundamental change. So don't stop with making the rational argument for your proposal. Take the next steps to overcoming resistance to change by casting your proposal in the light of the organization's culture. The Elders are the custodians of the Community's culture, which is the Founder's legacy. Visio and his friends were able to show how the Founder was on their side and that what they were proposing was actually what the Founder would do. You may not find a version of "the

Founder's book" so easily as Visio did, but there usually is an equivalent force you can add to your side. For example, simply casting your proposal as consistent with the organization's mission and a way to achieve some of the goals underlying the mission is a way to make it more palatable to higher level decision makers and make it more familiar. As Visio's fifth diary entry says, the most fearsome thing is the unknown. Being consistent with the existing mission removes some of the unknown and can make people less fearful about your proposal.

Another approach might be to co-opt an influential member of the organization to your cause, either at or above your level in the hierarchy. Regardless of whether the co-opted member gained influence through position or achievement, having him or her argue in favor of your proposal can sometimes make the difference. The point is, do not rely on allowing the data to stand alone so that any rational person will accept your proposal. What appears rational to you may not seem so to others. Understand your audience and tailor your proposal for that audience. Sometimes a mentor such as Mr. Philo, who has been around long enough to understand the politics and culture of the organization, can be a vital resource in understanding how to do this.

Whether it's the monster under the bed or the dragon in the closet or just the dark itself, many of us manifest a fear of the unknown left over from childhood. We shouldn't forget, however, that some children who fear the unknown also are very curious and sometimes undertake risks just to find out what is outside their usual domain. We usually outgrow our irrational fear of the unknown and sadly, in some cases, our curiosity, but there are often latent effects even among adults. For some adults, as Visio's fifth diary entry documents, the most fearsome thing is the unknown. The more light we can shed on our environment, the fewer unknowns exist to provoke irrational fear. Indeed, the unknown is often the most fertile ground for exploration to discover new opportunities. In diary entry number seven, Visio notes the importance of being open-minded about things that are new to us. Otherwise, new opportunities might be rejected out-of-hand as inconsistent with what we know and how we have always done things. Futurist Joel Barker characterized individuals as either explorers or settlers.[16] Explorers investigate the unknown and find new opportunities. Settlers follow the explorers to exploit the new discoveries. Of course, we need both explorers and settlers. Which are you? What is your organization's tolerance for explorers?

Visio's sixth diary entry reminds us that we can learn from failure, but as Matthew Syed,[17] the author of *Black Box Thinking*, also reminds us, many never do. And those failures to learn are related to Visio's seventh and eighth entries about being open-minded and about not allowing our fears to blind us to the potential good that might result from an encounter with the unknown. To take the eighth point first, think about "the blame game" that we all have played at one time or another. The blame for failure can be self-attributed ("Oh, what an idiot I am!") or attributed to "them and their shortcomings," and, since blame is often followed by punishment, no wonder we fear failure and cling to the comforting familiarity of the known and predicable. At times we even say things like "Better the devil we know than the devil we don't" to justify why we remain in a bad situation. (Think about it—if we don't know the other devil, then how do we know that he isn't really an angel?)

Let's contrast this with Visio and his friends. First, they were curious and the unknown was something to be explored, not simply feared. Thus, rather than putting him down, Visio's friends expanded his initial insight by gathering data to document the problem with the cheese supply. Second, when it came time for them to make their case to the Elders, they did not blame the Elders for their failure to understand the problem and see how grave it was. Imagine what response they would have gotten! Instead, they systematically analyzed the situation and proposed a positive response. Third, when their initial presentation failed to move the Elders into action, they did not blame the Elders or each other. They analyzed the reasons for their failure and then addressed them with the help of Mr. Philo.

Because of the way they handled themselves, the intrepid band had a chance to venture into the unknown territory on the other side of the door separating the Community from the maze. They became a band of prospectors, with a prospector's hope, optimism, and willingness to put up with bit of fool's gold along the way while searching for the mother lode.

Visio's eighth and twelfth diary entries remind us that there are risks associated with virtually everything we do—particularly endeavoring to create new cheese or reacting to a competitor who has created new cheese—to which you must react. But we cannot avoid taking action when needed because we are afraid of unknown or known risks. Risks should be identified and managed to the extent possible and weighed against the benefits of taking action. When the Community decided to enter into what amounts to a supply chain relationship with the Village, the Elders recognized that there was risk associated with trading an already scarce resource, cheese, for an unproven resource, milk. There was also the risk that the other community would steal the technology for making cheese. These were real risks in entering into this relationship, but there were also risks associated with doing nothing. Ultimately they decided to take action in a way that minimized the potential risks and maximized the potential benefits. Even if the eventual decision was that the risk of making change outweighs the risk of doing nothing, the organization is ahead of its previous state as a result of making the analysis.

Visio's ninth and tenth diary entries remind us to try to see the situation from the perspective of other people if we want to understand how they may act. That those in charge do not like public surprises is not surprising, once you place yourself in the position of someone in charge. When the surprise is public, the person in charge will feel pressured to make a decision on the spot. But most of us realize that one of the things decision-makers value greatly is keeping their options open, and presenting the surprise in private allows them to do that. Keeping the decision maker's perspective in mind can be a great help at "getting to yes," as in the title of Fisher and Ury's classic work.[18] The tenth diary entry is a reminder (consider Brutus' stab in the back) that other people— especially when the enterprise is risky and failure an option—may see the threats and opportunities *for themselves* in the situation in a very different light.

Let us take diary entry twelve next because it reminds us of the fallacy known as Appeal to Traditional Wisdom. The fallacy starts with reasoning that, because a course of action has worked for us in the past, we should continue on that same course. Obviously, in using this reasoning people are appealing to past success. And, to be certain, they have a point. The past success of a course of action is indeed an argument in favor of continuing it. But—and this is a big "but"—it may not make sense to continue on a course if (a) the circumstances have changed in a way that decreases the chances of repeating past success and/or (b) there is a new option available that has the promise of even greater success. There is nothing wrong with staying on course, provided you have spent some time and energy surveying the environment for relevant changes and actively engaged in looking for new ways to accomplish your goals. Of course, there is no guarantee that you will notice the changes in the environment or that you will discover the next new great thing, but it can be guaranteed that in a competitive environment others are actively working to change the environment and to bring in new ideas, and all of their activity may very well create the shoals on which a "steady as she goes" course founders. And, as Visio and his team discovered, the maze is always changing. What worked when the maze was configured in a particular way may not work at all in the maze's new configuration.

The eleventh diary entry noting that a debacle can be a source of opportunity may sound Pollyannaish. A *debacle* is defined as a complete failure, an utter rout in which what started as a disciplined army has now become a disorganized crowd of people running for their lives. How can such events be sources of opportunity? The answer is straightforward. If a debacle has occurred, then keeping to the *status quo* will have only a few advocates at most. The door is open, then, for a fundamental change in the way the organization does business. How many inspirational stories are there about a business that was about to go under that was saved by reinventing itself? There are stories old and new, from Lee Iacocca at Chrysler to Lou Gerstner at IBM and Steve Jobs returning to Apple. If people can keep their cool and if they have time for some serious thinking about what direction to take, then a debacle can be an opportunity.

Diary entry thirteen, about seeking out diverse experiences, fits very nicely with the evolving literature on personality traits. Adam Grant reports[19] on a study of the relationship between the arts and scientific success of Nobel Prize winning scientists that shows that the Nobelists were many times more likely than typical scientists to play an instrument, write poetry, do woodworking, or even perform as a dancer, actor, or magician. Robert McCrae notes[20] that the personality trait most associated with the arts is openness, and openness is conceived of being a combination of subtraits such as curiosity, introspection/depth/aesthetics, and the tendency to savor a variety of sensory experiences.[21] Visio notes in diary entry seven the importance of being open to new ideas and perspectives. Challenges that are unpredictable often need to be met with some creative thinking. The good news is that personality traits are not simply given; rather, deliberately engaging in creative activities is one way to foster openness, the aspect of one's personality that is most closely related to creative thinking.

Visio made diary entry fourteen after he and his friends ran into a solid wall on a trip to visit the Village, the source they had come to rely on for the milk that they turn into cheese. Remember what did *not* happen? The friends did not scurry about in a panic. They could have panicked because they knew full well that the wall was preventing them from accessing a resource that was absolutely vital. The milk from the Village had become the source of the Community's cheese supply, and they realized immediately that, if this problem was not solved, the Community's very existence was threatened.

Not only did they not panic, they also did not become immobilized by hopelessness. They did not treat this event as a total defeat. Yes, it was totally unexpected and unpredictable and yes, it presented a deadly threat, but their first response was to calmly analyze the situation. That analysis enabled Cassandra to have the fundamental insight "the maze changes," and for the team this was truly a "black swan,"[22] an unforeseeable, highly disruptive event. All of us rely on the mental maps that we have made of the reality that surrounds us; because those maps have functioned well for us in the past, all of us rely on them to tell us what is around the next corner. But we all know that, although a particular black swan event is unpredictable, in our fast-moving and interconnected world we will encounter one occasionally.

The question, then, is what can be done? The answer, in a word, is *resilience*. As the American Psychological Association (APA)[23] makes clear in its discussion of the resilience of people who have suffered deeply from a shock, resilience is not a property, it is a *process*. As the title of the APA booklet, "The Road to Resilience," makes clear, the process of resilience begins well before the disruptive event. In their summary of the psychological research they list "ten ways to build resilience," and here are the main ones:

- Make connections

- Avoid seeing crises as insurmountable problems

- Accept that change is a part of living

- Take decisive actions "rather than detaching completely from problems"

- Nurture a positive view of yourself "developing confidence in your ability to solve problems and trusting your instincts"

These pieces of advice have their counterparts for teams and organizations as well. Making connections means building relationships with people who can be trusted, who can be relied on in a pinch. These will be people who can be relied on to do what they say, to honor their commitments, and to be fully engaged in the process of working out a solution to the disruptive situation. The same character can be looked for in teams and organizations.

The point of caring about character is that we want to be able to rely on people in a crisis because they have the necessary skills and abilities. These are people who actively expand their horizons and who can put up with the demanding practice needed to become fluently skillful. This is part of what makes resilience a process, because the practice required ordinarily takes time spread out over days or weeks or maybe months. An obvious comparison is with a basketball team whose members spend the necessary time in the gym honing their skills so that they can be depended upon to execute the plays properly.

In addition to the organizational counterparts of the individual actions, from a more strictly organizational perspective there are two other bits of advice that may be surprising. Here are suggestions from Andrew Zolli,[24] the man who wrote the book on resilience (*Resilience: Why Things Bounce Back*):

1. The first suggestion is the paradoxical-sounding *"Don't maximize efficiency."* The point is to keep some resources in reserve to handle disruptive events. If there are no reserves, then the organization becomes "fragile'—liable to break when stressed. The need to keep some forces in reserve to initiate a counterattack seems to be a relevant military analogy. If you don't want your line of defense to be fatally compromised, you need to be able to mobilize reserves and direct them in a timely fashion to where they are most needed.

2. The second suggestion from Zolli is *"Don't forget about middle management."* As Zolli puts it, "When things go wrong, it's often people in the middle who determine an organization's resilience." To continue with the military analogy, how would an army perform if its NCOs were as green as the platoon commanders often are? Of course, Visio and his friends in our fable are precisely such people in the middle. They are people with skills and responsibility, but definitely not members of the Council of Elders. Yet they are the ones who are able to bring fundamental change to the Community's way of doing business.

TAKEAWAYS

So, what do we do differently as a result of having read the fable? Perhaps it would be useful to recast the lessons in this fable as questions you can ask about your organization and perhaps even yourself. The answers to these questions can help determine whether you and your organization are shapers of the future or simply pulled along by others who shape the future for you.

- Does your organization tend to be more reactive or proactive? Put another way, does your organization typically create its own change or does it merely react to change created by others—especially competitors? This is the main lesson of our fable. Some organizations have survived and indeed thrived by being good followers—allowing others to take the risks and staying nimble enough to catch up quickly. However, these are not the names we remember. The best organizations are the ones pushing against the boundaries and creating innovations and new paradigms. It isn't easy to be the one breaking new ground; however, it is usually more profitable and will better assure the long-term competitive position of the organization. In our fable, the long-term survival of the Community was only assured after they developed the courage to take control of their food supply. Rather than passively enjoying the cheese that the Founder had provided, they explored new territory, partnered with the Village, and used their ingenuity to create new cheese from the milk they obtained from the Village.

- Are you sagacious enough to recognize important things that simply pop up unannounced and that others miss? Visio was not looking for anything other than his cheese allowance when he noticed the vast empty space in the warehouse.

- When you identify a problem that others are not aware of, do you simply report it or do you also propose a course of action to deal with the problem? The easy thing for Visio to do once the Elders brushed him off was to wash his hands of the problem. After all, he did not occupy a position of authority. It wasn't his job to assure the supply of cheese. Had he done so, what would have been the fate of the Community?

- How do you react to negative feedback about a new idea when you propose it to friends and colleagues? Do you simply drop the idea, or do you try to take their feedback into account while persevering with developing the idea? Visio lost some friends who thought his plan was too bold. This is another point where it would have been easier for him to drop the whole thing and go back to being just plain Visio.

- How do you approach decision makers with ideas for change? Do you hope to let the facts speak for themselves, or do you attempt to understand your audience and what it will take to convince them of the need to change? Visio recognized the value of the Founder's book. It was better than, but no substitute for, the facts in convincing the Elders to accept his plan. Know your audience and what makes it tick.[25]

- Do you and your organization shrink from unknown territory and prefer to operate in an environment that is predictable and well understood? Or do you seize the chance to explore a new environment to see what valuable things you may find there? The Elders were firmly stuck in "the way of the Founder," or, put another way, "that's the way we have always done it." That had worked for many years and made their job easier. But the point was coming when "the way of the Founder" had to yield to new ways in order for the Community to survive.

- How does your organization react to failure? Does it punish failure or attempt to learn from it? How do you react to failure? Do you, like Thomas Edison, consider failure a quick way to learn, or do your shrink from the prospect of trying new things because you fear you might not succeed? Visio and his friends encountered many dead ends in the maze. At first these were viewed as failures. However, they eventually realized that with each dead end encountered and plotted on the map, they were learning more and more about the maze.

- What is the initial reaction of you and your organization to new things? Is it "that isn't the way we do things around here" or is it "hmmm, that is an interesting idea"? Does your organization manifest a "not invented here" mindset?

The Elders saw themselves as "all knowing and all wise" in the Community. They saw their job as making decisions according to their interpretation of what the Founder would have done. Upward communication was barely tolerated. After all, what could the Community members possibly know that the Elders didn't?

- Do you and your organization view the unknown future with fear or with excitement? Do you assess risk and balance it appropriately with the potential good that might result from your encounter with the unknown? Visio and his team entered fearfully into the maze. But while fearful, they persevered. Everyone feels fear of the unknown at some time. It is how you react to it that makes all the difference.

- Are you careful to keep management in the loop about ideas that may lead to transformative change? The Elders were more supportive when Visio and his friends kept them informed. Leaders do not like surprises. This is especially true when the surprises are sprung in public.

- Do you have a core group of colleagues whom you trust and whom you can use as sounding boards for your ideas? How do you react when one of these colleagues betrays your trust? Visio had a core group of friends, including Mr. Philo, that he trusted and with whom he could discuss anything. One of those friends betrayed that trust, but Visio did not let that stop him.

- Do you and your organization learn from your mistakes or simply attempt to fix blame and punish the guilty party? Visio's misplaced trust in Brutus led to Brutus gaining control over Visio's ideas. However, when Brutus's venture into the maze failed, Visio was prepared to learn from Brutus's mistakes and work to make the idea a reality.

- When you and your organization consider radical new ideas, do you assess the risk associated with doing nothing as well as the risk of pursuing the idea? The Community was unaware anyone else lived in the maze. Making a pact with the Village was very risky. "What if they come and steal what cheese we have left?" But the consequences of doing nothing were even more grave. "We run out of cheese and become like the Dead Community."

- Do you seek out the comfortable, predictable environment or do you value diversity? Does your organization encourage you to seek out varied experiences that can prepare you for dealing with unpredictable challenges? Visio's dance lessons seemed to have no conceivable purpose. It seemed just another way to fill time—like playing Angry Birds. Yet the strength and agility he gained were essential to his being able to climb the makeshift tower to survey his environment.

- Do you approach change by "planning the work" and "working the plan" or are you able to adapt your plan when things change? Visio had everything planned. Then the maze changed. A lesser person might have given up. Instead Visio, now the confident leader, gathered ideas from his team and formulated a new plan. A great general once said, "the plan is the plan until the first shot is fired." So it is in business as it is in war.

- How does your organization view the external environment within which it operates? Does it consider this environment to be largely static, assuming that what has always worked in the past will continue to work in the future? Or does it recognize that the environment is constantly changing and that those changes can represent both risks and opportunities? Does your organization constantly scan and assess its environment looking for these changes or is environmental scanning a perfunctory, seldom-used endeavor?

One big difference between our fable and Johnson's is that ours stresses the value of teamwork over individual action. But simply collecting a group of friends does not make them a team. Visio's team was diverse in a number of ways, and that diversity brought strength that enabled them to save the Community. As Stephanie Hill observes "It's a truism that the best teams are greater than the sum of their parts. I believe that is only true when those parts are diverse. When everyone looks the same, acts the same, and thinks the same, is it any wonder that they often fail to embrace—or even produce—innovative and unconventional ideas?"[26]

Wearing the same shirts doesn't make you a team.

— VINCE LOMBARDI

So, perhaps ours is not a trivial bit of fiction after all. Perhaps, too, the Community in our story should already be looking to create the next new cheese, because its current new cheese, like its old cheese, is unlikely to last forever.

References

American Psychological Association (APA). (2016). "Road to Resilience." Brochure from the APA Psychology Help Center found at http://www.apa.org/helpcenter/road-resilience. aspx.

Barker, J. (1990). *The Business of Paradigms.* Burnsville, MN: Charthouse International Learning Corp.

Beckett, S. (1983). *Worstward Ho!* New York: Grove Press.

Bloch, H. (2013). "Failure is an Option." *National Geographic* 224(3), p. 133.

Boyle, R. (2000). "Three Princes of Serendip." At http://livingheritage.org/three_princes.htm.

Clark, D. (2013). "5 Ways to Build a Resilient Organization" (interview with Andrew Zolli). *Forbes*, Feb. 28, 2013 at http://www.forbes.com/sites/dorieclark/2013/02/28/5-ways-to-build-a-resilient-organization/#7cbc7ac15424

Connelly, B., Ones, D., & Chernyshenko, O. (2014). "Introducing the special section on Openness to Experience: Review of openness taxonomies, measurement, and nomological net." *Journal of Personality Assessment, 96*(1), 1-16.

Fisher, R., & Ury, W. (2011/orig. 1991). *Getting to Yes.* New York, NY: Penguin Books.

Grant, A. (2016). *Originals: How Nonconformists Move the World.* New York, NY: Penguin Random House.

Griffin, A., R. Price, & B. Vojak. (2012). *Serial Innovators.* Stanford, CA: Stanford Business Books.

Hill, S. (2014). "In Pursuit of the Best Ideas." *Scientific American,* vol. 311, no. 4, pp. 48-49.

Houston Chronicle. (August 17, 2016), p. B2.

Johnson, S. (1998). *Who Moved My Cheese?* New York: G. P. Putnam's Sons.

Lewin, K. (1951). *Field Theory in Social Science.* New York: Harper & Rowe.

Lewin, K. (May 1943). "Defining the Field at a Given Time." *Psychological Review.* 50(3): pp. 292–310.

McCrae, R. (2007). "Aesthetic chills as a universal marker of openness to experience." *Motivation and Emotion* (2007) 31, 5-11.

Merton, R. & Barber, E. (2004). *The Travels and Adventures of Serendipity.* Princeton, NJ: Princeton University Press.

Motee, I. (2013). *Design Thinking for Strategic Innovation.* Hoboken, NJ: John Wiley & Sons.

Pascal, R. (1990). *Managing on the Edge.* New York: Simon and Schuster.

PricewatershouseCoopers. (2014) "Gut & Gigabytes: Capitalizing on the Art and Science in Decision Making." http://preview.thenewsmarket.com/previews/pwc/documentassets/345166.pdf.

Scott, A. (2014). "Cranking Up R&D." *Chemical & Engineering News* 92(1), 13-14.

Sower, V., & F. Fair. (2012). *Insightful Quality: Beyond Continuous Improvement.* New York: Business Expert Press.

Sower, V., & F. Fair. (2005). "There is More to Quality than Continuous Improvement: Listening to Plato." *Quality Management Journal* 12(1), 8-20.

Syed, M. (2015). *Black Box Thinking: Why Most People Never Learn from their Mistakes—but Some Do.* New York, NY: Penguin Random House.

Taleb, N. (2010). *The Black Swan: The Impact of the Highly Improbable* (2nd ed.) New York, NY: Random House.

Wallenberg, M. (2014) "The power of enduring companies." Interview with *McKinsey Quarterly* available at http://www.mckinsey.com/insights/Strategy/The_power_of_enduring_companies?cid=mckq50-eml-alt-mkq-mck-oth-1410&p=1.

Zolli, A. & Healy, A. (2012). *Resilience: Why Things Bounce Back.* New York, NY: Simon & Schuster.

About the Authors

D r. **Victor (Vic) Sower** is a Distinguished Professor Emeritus of Operations Management at Sam Houston State University (SHSU) and Partner Emeritus at Sower & Associates, LLC. At SHSU he taught courses in operations management, quality management, technology and innovation management, small business management, and supply chain management and established the Sower Business Technology Laboratory in the College of Business. He has also taught courses in Mexico and Germany. During his academic career he earned numerous awards for his teaching and research including the SHSU university-wide Excellence in Teaching award, the Excellence in Research award, and the Excellence in Service award and he was named a Piper Professor in 2005 by the Minnie Stevens Piper Foundation of Texas. He is the author of eight books and numerous journal articles and presentations.

Prior to entering academia, Vic served on active duty as an officer in the U. S. Army Chemical Corps and held a variety of positions in engineering, engineering management, and general management in industry. The characters in this fable are loosely based on composites from his business, academic, and consulting experience.

Dr. Frank Fair is Professor of Philosophy at Sam Houston State University (SHSU) where he has taught since 1971. In that time Frank has won the SHSU university-wide Excellence in Teaching award and the Excellence in Service award, and was named a Piper Professor in 2011 by the Minnie Stevens Piper Foundation of Texas. His list of courses taught includes Critical Thinking, Philosophy of Science, and a multi-year Honors Seminar on Decision-Making. Recently, inspired by the Philosophy for Children movement, Frank and a team of colleagues from SHSU conducted a study in the local public school system and documented a powerful cognitive effect of one hour per week structured discussions of philosophical ideas in seventh grade classrooms.

End Notes

1. Johnson, S. (1998).

2. Pascal, R. (1990).

3. Sower, V., & F. Fair. (2012).

4. Scott, A. (2014).

5. Sower, V., & F. Fair. (2012).

6. Beckett, S. (1983).

7. Bloch, H. (2013).

8. Lewin, K. (1951).

9. Lewin, K. (May 1943).

10. Sower, V., & F. Fair. (2012).

11. Sower, V., & F. Fair. (2012).

12. Griffin, A., R. Price, & B. Vojak. (2012).

13. *Houston Chronicle.* (August 17, 2016).

14. Wallenberg, M. (2014).

15. Boyle, R. (2000) and Merton, R. & Barber, E. (2004).

16. Barker, J. (1990).

17. Syed, M. (2015).

18. Fisher, R., & Ury, W. (2011/ orig. 1991).

19. Grant, A. (2016).

20. McCrae, R. (2007).

21. Connelly, B. et al. (2014).

22. Taleb, N. (2010).

23. APA (2016).

24. Clark, D. (2103) and Zolli, A. & Healy, A. (2012).

25. In a PricewatershouseCoopers research project (2014).

26. Hill (2014).

Index

Page numbers in *italics* refer to figures or tables.

The Knowledge Center
www.asq.org/knowledge-center

Learn about quality. Apply it. Share it.

ASQ's online Knowledge Center is the place to:

- Stay on top of the latest in quality with Editor's Picks and Hot Topics.

- Search ASQ's collection of articles, books, tools, training, and more.

- Connect with ASQ staff for personalized help hunting down the knowledge you need, the networking opportunities that will keep your career and organization moving forward, and the publishing opportunities that are the best fit for you.

Use the Knowledge Center Search to quickly sort through hundreds of books, articles, and other software-related publications.

www.asq.org/knowledge-center

TRAINING CERTIFICATION CONFERENCES MEMBERSHIP **PUBLICATIONS**

Ask a Librarian

Did you know?

- The ASQ Quality Information Center contains a wealth of knowledge and information available to ASQ members and non-members

- A librarian is available to answer research requests using ASQ's ever-expanding library of relevant, credible quality resources, including journals, conference proceedings, case studies and Quality Press publications

- ASQ members receive free internal information searches and reduced rates for article purchases

- You can also contact the Quality Information Center to request permission to reuse or reprint ASQ copyrighted material, including journal articles and book excerpts

- For more information or to submit a question, visit **http://asq.org/knowledge-center/ask-a-librarian-index**

Visit www.asq.org/qic for more information.

ASQ
The Global Voice of Quality®

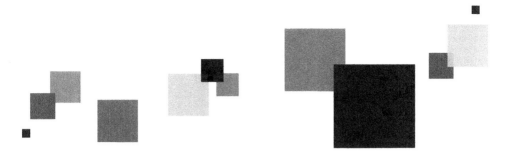

Belong to the Quality Community!

Established in 1946, ASQ is a global community of quality experts in all fields and industries. ASQ is dedicated to the promotion and advancement of quality tools, principles, and practices in the workplace and in the community.

The Society also serves as an advocate for quality. Its members have informed and advised the U.S. Congress, government agencies, state legislatures, and other groups and individuals worldwide on quality-related topics.

Vision

By making quality a global priority, an organizational imperative, and a personal ethic, ASQ becomes the community of choice for everyone who seeks quality technology, concepts, or tools to improve themselves and their world.

ASQ is...

- More than 90,000 individuals and 700 companies in more than 100 countries

- The world's largest organization dedicated to promoting quality

- A community of professionals striving to bring quality to their work and their lives

- The administrator of the Malcolm Baldrige National Quality Award

- A supporter of quality in all sectors including manufacturing, service, healthcare, government, and education

- YOU

Visit www.asq.org for more information.

ASQ
The Global Voice of Quality®

TRAINING CERTIFICATION CONFERENCES MEMBERSHIP **PUBLICATIONS**

ASQ Membership

Research shows that people who join associations experience increased job satisfaction, earn more, and are generally happier*. ASQ membership can help you achieve this while providing the tools you need to be successful in your industry and to distinguish yourself from your competition. So why wouldn't you want to be a part of ASQ?

Networking

Have the opportunity to meet, communicate, and collaborate with your peers within the quality community through conferences and local ASQ section meetings, ASQ forums or divisions, ASQ Communities of Quality discussion boards, and more.

Professional Development

Access a wide variety of professional development tools such as books, training, and certifications at a discounted price. Also, ASQ certifications and the ASQ Career Center help enhance your quality knowledge and take your career to the next level.

Solutions

Find answers to all your quality problems, big and small, with ASQ's Knowledge Center, mentoring program, various e-newsletters, *Quality Progress* magazine, and industry-specific products.

Access to Information

Learn classic and current quality principles and theories in ASQ's Quality Information Center (QIC), *ASQ Weekly* e-newsletter, and product offerings.

Advocacy Programs

ASQ helps create a better community, government, and world through initiatives that include social responsibility, Washington advocacy, and Community Good Works.

Visit www.asq.org/membership for more information on ASQ membership.

*2008, The William E. Smith Institute for Association Research

TRAINING CERTIFICATION CONFERENCES MEMBERSHIP **PUBLICATIONS**

The Global Voice of Quality®